NO PEEPING UNDER THE CURTAIN
Tips and Scripts for School Drama Productions

by
Gene Beck

The Scarecrow Press, Inc.
Metuchen, N.J., & London
1994

British Library Cataloguing-in-Publication data available

Library of Congress Cataloging-in-Publication Data

Beck, Gene. 1926–
    No peeping under the curtain : tips and scripts for school drama productions
/ by Gene Beck.
        p.   cm.
    Includes bibliographical references and index.
    ISBN 0-8108-2545-7 (alk. paper)
    1. College and school drama, American. 2. Amateur theater—United
States—Production and direction. 3. Drama in education—United
States   I. Title.
PN3178.P7B43   1994
371.3′332—dc20   93-40075

CONTENTS

PREFACE

It was indisputable. Greg was king. His stance, regal bearing, and authoritative voice made this totally believable. For those few fleeting moments the ragged jeans and stained T-shirt crammed into the crumpled grocery bag were forgotten. The role would never be.

Years later when we chance to meet, Greg, his eyes sparkling brightly, always confides, "I still remember the play we did when I was in your room!" And so, I have little doubt, do the others who were in that cast, or in any other.

Drama has a way of weaving unforgettable memories. The one art that encompasses all others: music, dance, design, journalism, and oral interpretation, it can easily be expanded to include history, psychology, and philosophy as well. When used in the classroom, drama can improve oral reading and aid comprehension; budding novelists and playwrights learn to have more logical plot development and characterization; and all types of literature can be enlivened and enriched through creative dramatization.

> Modern educational theatre is a creative activity which has personal and therapeutic values. Students develop such qualities as self-confidence, poise, cooperativeness, initiative, resourcefulness, self-control, self-discipline, and a sense of understanding and appreciation of the abilities and efforts of others. They learn the importance of systematic organization, orderly procedure, and detailed planning because even the most casual type of play production encourages and requires the development of organizational abilities. Students experience the feeling of belonging and they are provided with a controlled outlet for physical, emotional, and mental disturbances. . . . If students are shy, they are

taught to overcome shyness. If they are too aggressive, they
learn to temper aggressiveness with consideration for others.
Each of their needs is met because of the scope of compre-
hensiveness of the activities. Modern educational theatre is
a creative democratic activity where students, working
together in close harmony, learn the principles of democracy
and civic responsibility.[1]

This book contains practice exercises for the classroom, enrichment activities, large-cast plays, and step-by-step suggestions for
staging a successful production. It was written for the Gregs in
every class and to help you feel comfortable about incorporating
all facets of drama into your curriculum.

Let's face it. Although most people in theater would staunchly
deny the charge, drama, with all its ramifications, has nearly
ruined traditional classroom teaching! Gone are the days (if they
ever really existed) when students sat immobile, ready to digest
and remember each crumb of lore or learning that might be
forthcoming. They tune us out. There is simply no way a mere
mortal can constantly compete with the miracles of movies,
VCRs, video games, TVs, and *Star Trek.* The glamor and
excitement of show business is too much and we pale in compari-
son. The era of the always alert, instantaneously enthralled pupil
is no more.

That's the dilemma. The solution? Put theater on our side.
Make use of the undeniable attraction we all feel for the bright
lights and fantasy. Use it to spark imagination and make classrooms come alive. Drama can be incorporated to illustrate or
explain any lesson and make dull assignments exciting.

This manual is designed to help you do just that within its three
main parts. The first deals with drama in the classroom. Here the
teacher is given ways to help children learn to clarify their ideas,
think, imagine, and communicate. The procedures for using
creative dramatics are explained. Included are activities which
can be used in the classroom. They may also serve as examples of

---

1. F. Loren Winship, *Handbook for One-Act Plays.* Austin, TX: The University Interscholastic League, 1989, p. 2.

exercises which can be adapted for teaching other subjects. There are specific suggestions for implementing drama into other areas of the curriculum, and for training students to become competent speakers and actors.

The second section, entitled *10 Steps to a Super Production,* contains short, easy-to-read instructions that will help you present plays you are proud to have directed. Every aspect of a formal production is included. There are suggestions which range from how to present the most simple plays to methods of staging fairly complex ones. This section is designed to be used for reference and to help you feel comfortable and confident about your directing.

The third portion of the book contains dramatizations of fairy tales that children love. They were written to be given by or for children and can be presented in a classroom, puppet theater, or auditorium.

All plays are less than thirty minutes in length, so they can be used for assemblies, PTA programs, or be included in a billing of one-acts. The casts are large and instructions are given to modify them so every student in a class can have a role. Also included are discussion questions, topics for creative writing, and enrichment projects which can be done individually or by members of a group.

Included at the end of the book are a glossary and an index for quick reference.

Gene Beck
B.F.A. Drama Education
University of Texas at Austin

PART I:

DRAMA IN THE CLASSROOM

CREATIVE DRAMATICS

Theater is a natural outgrowth of human development. Children engage in dramatic activities when they play house, school, cowboys, or space explorers. It's one of the important ways they learn. When we incorporate drama into the curriculum we are simply taking advantage of its universal appeal. Creative dramatics are a direct outgrowth of observations of child's play.

Specifically, what is creative drama and how does it differ from traditional theater? In creative drama the participants are the primary creators. They engage in improvisations and spontaneous responses to situations of conflict. There is no finished performance before an audience and the teacher acts as a guide for evoking creative interaction.

Traditional theater starts with a play and a body of information to be learned. The leader is the expert who teaches specific skills, directs others in theater techniques, and makes the major decisions about the total production. Participants are the interpreters and their efforts culminate in a performance before an audience.

The two are similar because they involve learning how to manage relationships with others. They require actors to be uninhibited and self-disciplined and to understand what is being portrayed. In both, participants work for the benefit of the entire activity as well as for their individual contributions.[1]

---

1. Coleman A. Jennings, *Creative Drama and Theatre for Youth,* Drama 378/379 Handout. The University of Texas at Austin.

Procedures

Discipline

You should set a few guidelines before beginning any theater arts activity. Students need to be taught to stand perfectly still without speaking when a bell is rung or the word "freeze" is said. They need to know: 1) You will accept more noise in the classroom if they are involved in their tasks and ideas are flowing freely. 2) Others are laughing *with* them when they are performing, and under these circumstances the behavior is acceptable. 3) Everyone makes mistakes, including their teacher, and this is fine if we learn from our mistakes.

Begin with simple activities and expect your students to do their best. This will keep silliness to a minimum. If the class becomes a bit unruly, stop the activity and go to a calmer one. Your students will soon learn.

Seating Arrangements

Theater arts activities can be done at the front of any traditionally arranged classroom. I like to place desks in some variation of a "U" and have activities there. This allows room for freedom of expression and helps observers feel that they are a part of the action. The arrangement works well for teaching all areas of the curriculum and there are never any chairs to move when we begin dramatic activities.

The Warm-up Period

Creative dramatic activities are usually presented in a series of three steps. The first is the warm-up period when students become relaxed and receptive to the exercises which will follow. Rhythmic and musical activities are often used for this segment.

Warm-up Period Objectives: The learner will imitate sounds and perform singing games; develop body and spatial perceptions using rhythmic and interpretive movements; develop body and spatial perceptions using imitative movement; and employ active listening in a variety of situations.

Activities and Games:
1. Beat a rhythm by measures, usually six to eight beats, and have students reproduce the beats.
2. Have a student beat a rhythm and the rest of the class copy it.
3. Let students walk in a circle to the beat of a drum.
4. Change the drumbeat and have students march, skip, or hop to the beat of the rhythm.
5. Play a piece of music and have students clap, walk, and march keeping time to the music.
6. Sing peppy songs and have students pantomime the actions. Some examples are *When You're Happy and You Know It Give A Smile, I'm a Little Teapot, MacNamara's Band,* and *Here We Go Round the Mulberry Bush.* There are dozens of other songs that will work equally well.

Components of Creative Drama

The most frequently used forms of creative dramatics are these:

Sensory Awareness—Students are encouraged to use one or more of the five senses to interpret an experience imaginatively. The objectives are to heighten sensory awareness and perception.

Pantomime—Gesture, action, and movement without words.

Improvisation—The creation of a character through speech and movement. Students focus on becoming a person who thinks, feels, and reacts to a particular situation.

Story Dramatization—Students create an improvised story based on their imagination, literature, history, or current events.

During creative dramatics activities children need to be guided by an adult who assumes an active role for the presentations. To do this you can interject comments when the children are performing to keep them on task. This is called side-coaching. In the book *Theater Games for the Classroom,* Viola Spolin suggests using some of the following words and phrases:[2]

2. Viola Spolin, *Theater Games for the Classroom Grades 1-3.* Evanston, IL: Northwestern University Press, 1986.

Slow motion.	Use your back.
Look up.	Watch your hands.
Look down.	Use your full body.
Keep going.	Follow the leader.
Don't rush it.	Look all around you.
Watch your feet.	Work together.

Questions beginning with *what, when, why, how, which,* and *where* are also helpful.

Objectives for Creative Dramatic Activities: The learner will use pantomime, utilize improvisation, explore creative dramatization; develop vocal expression and experiment with dramatic interpretation; relate experiences with appropriate vocabulary in complete sentences.

Activities and Games:

1. Read a poem or short story to the class. Have the students stand by their desks and pantomime the action as it is being read. Judith Viorst's story, *Alexander and the Terrible, Horrible, No Good, Very Bad Day* works well, but any poem or short story with lots of action will do.
2. Discuss how our bodies show feelings. Have the students contribute their ideas and demonstrate.
3. Have students pantomime each of the following situations. At the end of each enactment ask for ways the scene could have been made better.

Eating	Putting on shoes
Drinking	Applying makeup
Sewing	Planting a flower
Dozing	Reading a book
Flying	Getting dressed
Marching	Taking a bath
Dancing	Patting the dog
Tasting hot soup	Testing bath water

Smelling flowers	Riding a bicycle
Stirring a pan	Driving a car
Eating ice cream	Smelling smoke
Trying on shoes	Brushing teeth
Directing a band	Smelling garbage
Eating a pickle	Putting on perfume

4. Let each student in the class suggest an activity such as the ones above and select another student to demonstrate it.
5. Have students work in small groups to dramatize a short story. They will need an opportunity to plan the action before presenting it to the class. The following are fun and easy to do: *The Three Bears, The Three Billy Goats Gruff, Little Red Riding Hood,* and *The Three Little Pigs.*

Quieting or Cool-Down Activities

Educational dramatics should end quietly. This will help students return to schoolwork more rested and at a slower pace. As a hint, try to schedule this time immediately prior to lunch or recess, or when students move to another locale. This way your children will have the opportunity to unwind on their own. The following exercises provide concrete examples of relaxation techniques and methods of handling stress.

Quieting Activities: All instructions should be given in a calm, low-pitched voice. Have students close their eyes while listening. Quiet music played in the background is helpful. Humperdinck's *Evening Prayer* or Schumann's *Traumerie* are both effective.

1. Have students get their bodies tense, then relax each area as they are told: feet, ankles, knees, legs, arms, stomach, and neck.
2. Tell pupils to alert their minds, then relax their bodies. Give the following instructions: "Take long, deep breaths. Pretend there are holes in the bottoms of your feet. Imagine good, warm feeling coming into your feet and gradually

filling your body. Think of the nicest thing you can imagine. Relax. Take deep breaths.''

3. Tell students to pretend they are leaves floating in water, clouds high in the sky, sand castles being washed away by waves, or snowmen slowly melting.

USING CREATIVE DRAMATICS TO TEACH OTHER SUBJECTS

Every teacher is well aware of the necessity and value of drill in the classroom. It is essential. It can also be boring. Remember we are competing with high-tech video games and science fiction movies. No wonder our students often tune us out. There is an answer, however. By implementing dramatics we can make the ordinary classroom a place where exciting things happen.

The essential elements teachers are required to teach in every subject are so closely related in the language arts and drama areas that some are interchangeable. This makes it easy to modify many of the activities you can find for theater and use them to teach two lessons at once. You can reap the rewards of creative dramatics and at the same time be teaching that English lesson you know they also need. When you do this, a revitalizing of the curriculum can happen. Your children will be learning and having fun at the same time, which is, of course, the way school should be!

The following exercises are designed to teach capitalization, punctuation, parts of speech, and subject and predicate. By using your imagination you can adapt them to teach these or other objectives that are appropriate to the grade level as well.

With each play in the third section of the book, you will find numerous suggestions for implementing activities which apply to all the humanities, research (dramaturgy), social studies, creative writing, and art. Although designed specifically for a particular story, the ideas may be adapted for other dramas or types of literature.

Teaching Grammar

Objectives: The student shall be provided opportunities to use the fundamentals of grammar and punctuation; use correct forms of nouns, verbs, and modifiers (adjectives and adverbs); produce basic sentence patterns and variations; and use subject-verb agreement in person and number.

Capitalization

1. Warm-up: As rapidly as possible call out a mixture of common and proper nouns, e.g., girl, Bob, city, month, December, Chicago. As soon as each word is said have the students say either proper noun, common noun, or capital letter, small letter.
2. Give a simple sentence, like "I can see Toni." Repeat it, having students either individually or in a group raise a hand each time a word should be capitalized.
3. Have students write sentences with at least one proper noun. Ask a group of three or four children to stand in front of the class. The child writing the sentence reads it twice. Performing students squat down for common nouns and stand up for proper ones. Ask the one reading the sentence if the motions were correct. Give a point to the team if everyone was right. The team with the most points wins.

Punctuation

1. Warm-up. Say a sentence to the class twice, such as, "Is it raining?" Students should call out the proper punctuation for the ending of the sentence.
2. Divide the class into two teams. Read a sentence twice. The second time have the students raise their hands in a circle over their heads for a period, hold them straight for an exclamation point, hold one hand up bent at the wrist for a question mark. If everyone on the team gives the correct

response the team will get a point. This may also be done with individual team members.

3. Repeat the procedures for Activity #2, adding commas, quotation marks, semicolons, apostrophes, etc. Commas are shown with a bent arm at the side, quotations marks with both arms bent, parallel to each other. An apostrophe is made like a comma, but with the arm raised. A colon is both fists raised, one above the other. A semicolon is a fist above a curved hand.

4. Instruct the students to write a sentence. Each child reads his sentence to either an individual or a group, who then shows the punctuation marks in the way suggested in Activity #3. The reader tells if the punctuation is correct.

Parts of Speech

1. Warm-up: Tell the class that they are going to learn the difference between a noun and a verb. Explain that a noun is the name of a person, place, or thing and a verb is an action word. Call out words such as *walk, baby, sit, cry, squirrel,* etc., or show them on flashcards. Students must say either "noun" or "verb" after each word is said.

2. Put the following words on small slips of paper and place them in a container. Let students take turns drawing a noun and then pantomiming it in front of the class. Do side-coaching and set a time limit of thirty seconds or a minute. Other students in the class may guess the name of the noun being enacted.

teacher	mechanic	student
doctor	fairy	witch
father	carpenter	queen
farmer	fisherman	bus driver
horse	book	airplane
room	seesaw	bird
nurse	baby	clown

artist	painter	lion tamer
mother	cook	king
custodian	child	police officer
tree	chair	wheelbarrow
cave	clock	bicycle

3. Tell the students that an adjective describes or modifies a noun. Use the procedures for Activity #4 and have the students pantomime the following adjectives:

sleepy	brave	afraid
angry	happy	excited
ashamed	helpful	mean
lazy	crazy	confused
flirtatious	scholarly	dreamy
sick	sad	unhappy
hungry	tired	curious
kind	loving	shy
rude	amused	disgusted
annoyed	nervous	impatient

Be sure to use the word "adjective" as many times as possible to reinforce the lesson being taught.

4. Show the students how adjectives can compare, as in "small, smaller, smallest" and "big, bigger, biggest." Divide the class into groups of three. Have each team decide on an adjective to compare and then show it to the class.
5. Place slips of paper with the names of nouns in one container and the names of adjectives in the other. Have students draw one noun and adjective from each stack and then demonstrate the words they have drawn for the class.
6. Repeat the procedures for Activity #5 using nouns and verbs.
7. Let the students draw the name of an adjective from a container. Have them change the adjective to a noun and

pantomime that word. Examples might be "sleepy to sleep," "sick to sickness," "shy to shyness."

8. Repeat the procedures for Activity #7, changing adjectives to adverbs.

9. Tell the class that adverbs modify or describe verbs. They tell *how, when,* or *where.* Let students work in pairs and show an adverb and verb. Examples might be "walked slowly," and "ran fast." One student should be the verb and the other the adverb.

10. Tell the students that they are going to play a game using adverbs and verbs. Select one player to be "it" who then leaves the room. Blindfold the player outside the room. Then place objects in the playing space, such as a book, chairs, wastebasket, etc. Select a second player to be the director. The object of the game is to see if the director can walk the blindfolded student through the objects without touching them while using only verbs and adverbs. Instructions might go like this: "Crawl slowly," "Stop fast," "Turn right." If the director says a word other than a verb and adverb, the other students should raise their hands. The student who catches the director in an error becomes the new director. No two directions may be the same.

Subject and Predicate

1. Warm-up: Explain to the class that today they will learn about subjects and predicates. Tell them that a subject tells what the sentence is about and a predicate tells what happens to the subject. Give the students the subject of a sentence and then point to someone to supply a predicate, as in "The cat" . . . "ran into the house." Go through this procedure as rapidly as possible.

2. Let students choose a partner and enact a sentence. One person can be the subject and the other the predicate. Other members of the class try to guess the sentence.

3. Have each student make up a sentence and enact it. The first student to guess the sentence and tell the subject and predicate is the next to perform.

Teaching Phonics

The sound-symbol relationship taught in phonics classes is the basis for most reading programs. Knowing the sound each letter, digraph, diphthong, and blend represents most of the time is a valuable decoding skill which helps reading make sense for a large percentage of students. Understanding the meanings of prefixes and suffixes aids comprehension. Learning this information requires practice and drill. The following objectives lend themselves well to creative dramatics activities.

Phonics Objectives: The learner will discriminate letters; discriminate sounds for each letter of the alphabet; use basic phonic analysis for initial blends/digraphs/diphthongs; use complex structural analysis: root words/common affixes/contractions; alphabetize according to two or more letters; and use complex phonic analysis including initial clusters/medial diphthongs/digraphs.

1. Warm-up: Use a stack of five or six flashcards. Show the cards as rapidly as possible, changing the order often. Have the class call out the name of the letters or sounds. This exercise works well with vowels, consonants, digraphs, blends, or diphthongs.
2. Seat the students in a circle. Have the first student say the letter "a" and give a word starting with that letter. The second student must repeat the word starting with "a" given by the initiator and add a word starting with "b." Continue around the circle in the same manner. If a student is unable to remember a word, play goes to the next child. As the class becomes more proficient in alphabetizing, add two or three words per letter, insisting that they be placed in order.

3. Divide the class into two teams. Students take turns giving words that rhyme to members of the other team: "at, bat, cat, fat, gnat, hat, mat, pat, rat, sat, slat, that, vat." When a team member fails to think of a new word, the other team gets a point.

4. Divide the class into several small groups. Have a team member draw a letter or combination of letters to be illustrated with a pantomime given by each team member simultaneously. For example, the letters "sh" are drawn. Students might pantomime "shoe," "show," "shake," and "sharp." The first member of an opposing team to say all four words correctly and give the letters making the beginning sounds gets to draw next for the team, and the game proceeds.

5. Seat students in a circle. Build a story by having each child in the circle give a sentence starting with the next letter of the alphabet. The story might go like this: *A*lice was a little alligator. *B*ut Alice wasn't happy. *C*ody was Alice's best friend. *D*ay after day they would play together. *E*very day they would argue. When a player is unable to give a sentence with the proper letter, the next player takes the turn.

Teaching Science, Health, Safety

"Traditionally, schools have been very left-hemisphere brain oriented, often at the expense of learning approaches that include or emphasize right-hemisphere attributes. Theatre arts offer experiences in which both hemispheres can play major roles."[1] When we utilize this factor we add another dimension to our instruction and strengthen our teaching techniques.

In the lower grades science, health, and safety are often grouped together and a single grade given. For this reason

---

1. June Cottrell, *Creative Drama in the Classroom Grades 1–3*. Lincolnwood, IL: National Textbook Co., 1987, p. 81.

objectives are combined here. Numerous creative dramatics activities work well for teaching these subjects, particularly on a
primary level. A few are given here. There are many others.

Objectives: The student shall be provided opportunities to
know the senses; learn the seasons of the year; use comparisons:
length, area, shape, height, size, texture, and color; practice
safety; identify practices that promote: health, cleanliness, good
posture, and nutrition; and recognize the causes of communicable
diseases.

1. Have the students illustrate each of the senses with a
   pantomime, for example, eating an ice cream cone, reading
   a book, smelling a flower.
2. Let the students act out activities that are popular during
   each season of the year.
3. Working as individuals or teams, students can demonstrate
   proper grooming and cleanliness procedures, e.g., brushing
   teeth, bathing, cleaning hands, nails, feet.
4. Have students work in groups to develop skits illustrating
   safety on the playground, on the street, and at home.
5. Working as teams, the students can devise pantomimes or
   skits which demonstrate how communicable diseases are
   spread.

Teaching Math

In math, like science, there are many creative drama exercises
which can be used to enliven and enrich the subject on an
elementary level. A few are given here as examples; you will be
able to think of additional ones. Activities given in other sections
of this chapter may also be adapted to use in this area for other
objectives.

Objectives: Students shall be provided opportunities to add,
subtract, multiply, and divide whole numbers; solve problems by
selecting and matching strategies to given situations; use mea-

surement units of money, time, length, weight/mass, and temperature; and recognize and name geometric shapes.

1. Let the students work as teams and use their bodies to construct geometric shapes.
2. Let students apply measurements to the construction of puppets and puppet stages.
3. Tell the students to bring empty boxes and cans for a grocery store in your room. Let children make purchases with play money.
4. Set up a restaurant in your classroom. Coffee shops and restaurants often have old menus they haven't thrown out and are willing to give them away for the asking. Have the students take turns ordering, taking orders, and paying the bill. (Figuring the tip is optional depending upon the level of your students.)
5. Have students act out story problems.

TRAINING STUDENTS TO BECOME EFFECTIVE ACTORS AND SPEAKERS

Poised, controlled, self-confident people are universally admired. We dub them "winners" and watch them develop during their school years as they are elected to offices and receive honors. Ultimately they become our heads of state, our diplomats, the directors of corporate businesses, our civic leaders, and our officers in local organizations. They are the ones who shape our destiny.

We tend to think of people as having been born with these attributes. More often than not the traits which appear to be the result of natural personality are developed. Speaking in front of a group is one of the ways it is done. It builds self-confidence and aids in the accurate communication of facts and ideas.

Psychologists tell us shy persons usually do not get what they want and consequently do not feel good about themselves. It is important to stand tall, speak up, look others in the eye, and communicate feelings and ideas. When we play the role of someone else and get outside of ourselves it is often much easier to do. For this reason alone training in acting is important.

In his book *Psycho-Cybernetics,* Dr. Maxwell Maltz says that self-image is the key to human personality and human behavior, and that by expanding on this image we increase the area of the possible. He further states that self-image can be changed by applying creative imagination. "The method itself consists in learning, practicing, and experiencing new habits of thinking, imagining, remembering, and *acting* in order to develop an adequate and realistic self-image. . . . It is role-playing, which is simply picturing yourself in various situations, then solving them in your mind until you know what to do and say whenever the situation comes to real life. . . ."[1]

When we as teachers implement drama in our classrooms we are giving our students the tools to use as Dr. Maltz suggests, and the practice and experience to use them well. I have seen the amazing differences they can make. I have watched some of the shyest students become the best, most outgoing speakers at the end of a few months. I have seen their eyes start to sparkle and their confidence grow as they observe the admiration and respect of peers. I have watched them gain acceptance into social groups that were previously closed to them. I have seen them get major roles in plays and programs year after year. They have been taught to think on their feet and communicate their ideas and feelings.

I have seen shy, introverted adults come into Community Theatre groups when they were so self-conscious and retiring that speaking to new acquaintances was an obvious effort. I have watched them go from backstage crews to minor, then major roles in productions. I have observed attitudes change and self-confidence develop as their self-images were altered and they came to look on themselves not as losers but as winners. I have seen these same people move on to more productive and better-paying jobs. When we allow drama to come into our classroom we are affording our students the same opportunities. We are giving the magical keys to success.

There are four components of acting: body movement, voice, listening, and characterization. They are obviously interdependent. For our purposes we shall briefly discuss each of these integral parts and then give some activities for their development and improvement at the end of each section.

---

1. Maxwell Maltz, M.D., F.I.C.E., *Psycho-Cybernetics*. New York: Pocket Books—A Division of Simon and Schuster, 1960.

Controlling the Body in Front of an Audience

We've all seen speakers whose hands, feet, and body movements were so distracting we paid no attention to what was being said. Hands were moving jerkily and frantically about for no apparent reason or appeared to be glued to the inside of pockets. Feet shuffled uncomfortably, and weight shifted from one foot to the other. Shoulders were slumped and head and eyes often looked to the floor or around the sides of the room. All the body seemed to be saying was, "I'm uncomfortable being here and I hope I can get this over with as soon as possible!" The audience was certainly in agreement.

Control of the body while speaking in front of a group of people is the first step in acting. This is really not too difficult and once this is mastered the other components of acting start to fall into place naturally. The trick is to start slowly, and concentrate on one thing at a time. The goals are for the actor or speaker to be in complete control of the body at all times, and for good eye contact to be maintained between the speaker and the audience and between conversing actors on stage.

Suggestions for Teachers

Objectives: The student shall be provided opportunities to speak to accomplish a variety of purposes: informing, persuading, and entertaining; use a variety of words to express feelings and ideas; speak clearly, at an appropriate rate, and with proper sequencing; make organized oral presentations, and explain how to do something; and use language to comment on personal experience and for self-representation.

Activities and games: Whether you are teaching in a lower grade self-contained classroom or in a secondary class, you can start training your students to become poised actors or actresses from the first day of school without their even knowing it. Of course, this will make a difference in the plays you present, but more importantly, what a gift you will have given your students! Here's how to get started:

Day 1: Initially, everyone wants to know something about everyone else in the class, and there is no better way to get acquainted than to have students introduce themselves. This time, however, start raising your standards. Insist that students go to the front of the room, say their names, then, if possible, tell a little bit more about themselves. Model. Show them how to do it. The big thing is to get students talking in front of a group. This is enough for the first day. Keep it light and pleasure-filled.

Day 2: Your objective can be to have the learners walk with head up, giving the appearance of confidence, to the front of the room to say their names.

Day 3: The learners will walk to the front of the room with poise. They will pause, and while keeping feet still and hands out of pockets, look into the faces of the audience and say their names.

Day 4: Students repeat the previous exercises. Pause, give names, pause, standing completely still, then return to seat with confidence and poise.

Day 5: As above, but this time add a second statement, and each ensuing day add another. Some suggestions are as follows:

I go to . . . School.
I ride bus number. . . .
I am . . . years old.
My teacher's name is. . . .
I have . . . brothers and . . . sisters.
My mother's name is. . . .
My father's name is. . . .
I like to watch TV. My favorite show is. . . .
I like it because. . . .

Before you or the students are really aware of what is happening, they have become relaxed speaking in front of a group, and are giving long talks. As students begin feeling more and more comfortable doing this and want to say more, it is usually necessary to cut each person's ''show and tell'' time down to once a week, but this is enough to maintain the standards you've set and it gives ample time to review them. Divide the class into five groups and assign each group a day in which they do this. It won't take long and will be well worth the effort. Students actually start to look forward to talking to the class, and as they become more relaxed they can be given the option of other topics.

Be sure to insist that all wiggles and giggles be eliminated by having students start over if they occur. It's really surprising how fast students become relaxed in front of a group when trained this way. You're going to take great pride in your excellent young speakers, too!

It has been my experience that, contrary to the widely held notion of telling students to look above the heads of the audience to make them relax when speaking to a group, the opposite actually happens. A terrifying blur is created and stage fright becomes much worse! Instead of this, instruct students to take a deep breath, smile, and look into the faces of their friends just as they would do in normal conversation.

When this is done communication really begins. The speaker starts to watch to see if others are understanding what is being said. The emphasis changes from self to others and stage fright disappears. Who knows how many better jobs have been won just because of this basic exercise?

The Voice

When a role is well played, each word an actor speaks can be heard by every member of the audience at all times. The voice is controlled, pitch and inflections are varied, and every line creates the illusion that it's being given for the first time. All dialogue is said in a natural, convincing way and is never "sing-songy," stilted, or appearing to be memorized. The timbre, or tone of the voice, is pleasant, and unless deliberately changed for characterization, the tones are rounded and resonant. Rate of delivery is varied and pauses effectively used.

Suggestions for the Teacher

Objectives: The learner will use voice to explore thought, feeling, and role in dramatic activities; use voice as a means of self-expression; and identify and use vocal techniques to express a variety of characterizations.

Activities and Games

1. Have students take a deep breath and then count orally to see how high they can count without taking another breath.
2. Practice inhaling and exhaling deeply while making a continuous *Ho-oooooooo* sound and taking twenty-five steps.
3. Have students practice holding their breath while you or someone else counts.
4. Help the students learn to say tongue twisters accurately and with speed:

Around the rugged rock, the ragged rascal ran.
She sells seashells by the seashore.
Peter Piper picked a peck of pickled peppers. A peck of pickled peppers Peter Piper picked. If Peter Piper picked a peck of pickled peppers, where's the peck of pickled peppers Peter Piper picked?

5. Have pupils practice saying the same line with different inflections:

I like him. I *like* him. I like *him*.
Why did you do that? Why *did* you do that? Why did *you* do that? Why did you *do* that? Why did you do *that*?
Do you like spinach? Do *you* like spinach? Do you *like* spinach? Do you like *spinach*?

These are all good warm-up exercises. Others of similar types can be added.

Listening

"Active listening is a most important element of acting. When another actor is speaking the silent actor should: 1) Listen carefully. 2) React to the idea of the speaking actor. 3) Think of his idea in reply. 4) Take a breath. 5) Speak on cue."[2]

This aspect of drama provides good practice for students by teaching them to show respect and consideration for the ideas and feelings of others. It helps them listen, predict, and understand. These are areas of the communication process that are most often overlooked in language arts procedures.

Suggestions for Teachers
Objectives: The student will be provided opportunities to respond to nonverbal clues; respond to a speaker by asking questions and contributing information; listen to identify the main idea of a speaker's message; employ active listening in a variety of situations.

Activities and Games
The following activities develop listening skills and help students practice reacting with appropriate facial expressions while another actor talks.

1. Assign partners. Have students practice at their seats first, then give the dialogues in front of the class:

A: You're late.	**A:** I brought you something.
B: I know. I couldn't help it.	**B:** You did? What is it?
A: I'm still very angry.	**A:** You'll have to open it.
B: I was afraid you would be.	**B:** I can't wait.
A: You should have called me.	**A:** I hope you like it.
B: Next time I will.	**B:** I bet I will.

---

2. Alexander Dean and Lawrence Carra, *Fundamentals of Play Directing.* New York: Holt, Rinehart and Winston, 1974, p. 52.

2. Have students write other six-line dialogues and practice them the same way.

Characterization

Good characterization requires the actor to truly understand the person being portrayed. For each line that is delivered there should be an answer to each of these questions: (1) *How* can this be convincingly said? Would it be spoken rapidly or slowly? Should there be pauses? (2) *Why* is this line said? Is it for humor? To add suspense? Is it for character development? (3) *Which* word or words should be given particular emphasis? Which sentences in a longer dialogue? (4) *When* should the line be given? Should it be immediately after the cue, or should there be a deliberate pause? (5) *Where* should I be standing when I give the line? Where are my hands and feet? (6) *What* can I do to give the speech more effectively? What would the character be thinking about when saying the speech? These are the types of questions that the teacher/ director can ask the actors to help them give more effective characterizations.

In acting, as in all phases of dramatic activity, teamwork should be stressed. Students must learn to help and encourage one another. They should never be allowed to giggle or laugh if someone makes a mistake. Caustic comments should be avoided at all costs. An attitude of friendliness and cooperation keeps things pleasant and fun. One of the ways of achieving this is by asking questions of the cast. For example: What are your ideas on the subject? Can you think of another way to improve this? How can we make it better?

There are a few finer points on acting that should be touched on briefly: first, listening for the laughter of the audience and holding or freezing until it has stopped. This appears perfectly natural on stage and keeps lines from going unheard. The second concerns

entering and exiting in character. Few sights are as strange as that
of a queen walking in like a self-conscious beggar woman, then
suddenly assuming a regal stance as she says her first line. Heads
should always be up so the audience can see faces. Mistakes and
forgotten lines can escape detection if the actor making them
gives no bodily indication and each member of the cast has been
taught to say the cue line of the erring person and then give his
own. This takes a little practice but even first graders can do it,
given instructions and experience.

Timing is most important. Subtle changes in voice, pitch,
tempo, and volume add polish and interest. Pauses can be most
effective.

All movement needs to be planned and you need to watch
carefully to see that everyone who is not giving lines is keeping
still. Any on-stage movement attracts attention and is called
"stealing." It detracts from the action of the play, as the name
implies, so keep an alert eye open for feet swinging from a chair
or hands scratching heads! An actor who is blocked by moving
and cannot be seen by everyone in the audience should very
slowly and quietly shift position and move unobtrusively to avoid
being blocked. This is called "dressing stage." These points are
covered in more detail in the section entitled "Methods of
Staging" in the *10 Steps to a Super Production* section of the
book.

One final point: play down nervousness. Assure your actors
that they have rehearsed until they know exactly what to do,
and so everything is going to be fine. They're going on auto-
matic pilot! Explain that some nervousness is good. It is
what makes outstanding performances. No one wants to watch
people looking bored on stage. Controlled nervousness is what
is important and this comes with rehearsal. It is also what makes
a play good.

Suggestions for the Teacher
Objectives: The learner will use movement techniques for
characterization activities; use movement and imagination to

express thought, feeling, and character; and use imagination in character development.

Activities and Games

1. Give each student in the class one of these activities to perform at the front of the room. Other class members can guess who the performers are and what they are doing:

A boxer coming into the room.
A girl wearing her first pair of high heels.
A football player coming onto the field.
A person crossing a room in very tight shoes.
Someone looking for something that has been dropped.
Someone who is very frightened.
A person who has just made a batch of cookies for a friend.
A child walking down a road stepping over puddles.
A dog owner calling a dog to come home.
A child who is lost.
A person selling tickets.
A child being sent to the principal's office.
A student with a stomachache.
A teacher seeing a student cheating.
A mother who is angry because her vase was broken.
A store owner sweeping the sidewalk.
A very tired person getting ready for bed.
Someone who is late.
A person who is early.
Someone who is feeling nervous.
A teenager trying on a new outfit.
A player going up to bat at a baseball game.
A very tall person getting ready to bowl.
A happy person going to a movie.

2. These exercises will improve the students' acting and oral interpretation as well. Have them practice the following:

I hate you.	You broke it.
My head aches.	He's coming after me!
I'm so afraid.	I can't move!
Watch out.	I ruined it!
I love you.	I understand.
I feel terrible.	I'm so angry.
This is wonderful!	I'm lost!
My throat is sore.	I'm sorry.
My feet hurt.	Do we have to go?
I'm so sleepy.	He hates me.
Get out this minute!	I think she really likes me.
Leave me alone.	

3. Students can work in pairs and develop dialogues for the following situations. They should practice at their seats first, then give the dialogues in front of the class:

You've just broken a window and the owner sees you.
You are lost and ask directions.
You are in a store and break a dish.
You are late and your mother is very angry.
Your teacher takes points off for a mistake you didn't make.
You want your mother to let you go somewhere.
Your father is angry because you did not empty the garbage.
Your friend has just said something that hurt your feelings.
You have been asked to be a buddy to a new student at school.
A stranger approaches you and wants you to come with him.
You've just seen a robbery.

4. Have students work in pairs to develop their own dialogues to present to the class.

BIBLIOGRAPHY FOR PART I

This is the first of two annotated bibliographies. It contains references to information discussed in the previous section of the book. The bibliography for Part II is located immediately following that section. The resource listings included there pertain to staging a play.

Allstrom, Elizabeth. *Let's Play a Story.* New York: Friendship Press, 1966, fifth printing. Written primarily for young elementary school children, it is easily read and contains excellent suggestions for all aspects of drama in the classroom.

Bauer, Caroline Feller. *Handbook for Storytellers.* Chicago: American Library Association, 1977. A valuable book for helping oral language development, it contains good suggestions for creative drama as well.

Caldwell, Louise. *How to Guide Children.* Nashville, TN: Convention Press, 1981. A book loaded with enrichment activities for drama, art, and research.

Carlile, Clark. *38 Basic Speech Experiences.* Caldwell, ID: The Caxton Printers, 1982. 7th revised edition. An excellent book containing information about the various types of speeches, suggested topics, and basic fundamentals of speaking.

Cottrell, June S. *Creative Drama in the Classroom.* Lincolnwood, IL: National Textbook Co., 1987. Contains the theories and rationale for creative dramatics and suggestions for its implementation. Good, workable teaching plans are also given.

Furness, Pauline. *Role-Play in the Elementary School.* New York: Hart Publishing, 1976. Contains fifty role-play lesson plans with an emphasis on problem-solving.

Heinig, Ruth Beall. *Creative Drama Resource Book, Kindergarten Through Grade 3.* Englewood Cliffs, NJ: Prentice Hall, 1987. Easily read and has excellent suggestions for pantomimes, improvisations, songs, and games.

McCaslin, Nellie. *Creative Drama in the Primary Grades.* New York: Longman, 1987. Professor McCaslin reminds us that dramatic activities in the classroom are not frills but an essential component of the curriculum. Games and activities are included, along with a very good section on puppet construction and manipulation.

―――. *Creative Drama in the Intermediate Grades.* New York: Longman, 1987. Contains good information on traditional theater and some skits and scenes from plays. Basic principles of play production and creative dramatics also included.

McIntyre, Barbara M. *Creative Drama in the Classroom.* Itasca, IL: Peacock, 1974. Shows how creative drama can be successfully used to supplement language arts programs.

Polette, Nancy, and Marjorie Hamlin. *Celebrating with Books.* Metuchen, NJ: Scarecrow Press, 1977. Has valuable suggestions for enrichment activities which can be used in conjunction with educational theater in the classroom.

Salisbury, Barbara. *Theatre Arts in the Elementary Classroom, Kindergarten Through Grade Three.* New Orleans: Anchorage Press, 1986. A book designed to be useful to teachers with limited experience in using drama in the classroom. It contains objectives, activities, and many stories and poems to dramatize.

Schwartz, Dorothy, and Dorothy Aldrich, eds. *Give Them Roots . . . and Wings!* New Orleans: Anchorage Press, 1986, 2nd edition. Written in workbook form, this text contains goals, activities, and evaluation checklists of value to teachers.

Siks, Geraldine Brain. *Drama with Children.* New York: Harper & Row, Inc., 1983, 2nd edition. Written specifically for children, the book contains exercises which are appropriate for older students as well.

Spolin, Viola. *Theater Games for the Classroom: Grades 1-3.* Evanston, IL: Northwestern University Press, 1986. A teacher's handbook packed with suggestions for making learning fun.

―――. *Theater Games for the Classroom: Grades 4-6.* Evanston, IL:

Northwestern University Press, 1986. A continuation of activities for older children. Includes some production suggestions.

Tanner, Fran Averett. *Creative Communication.* Caldwell, ID: Clark Publishing Co., 1979. An extremely useful book for teaching acting, speaking, and oral reading. Has excellent projects.

Ward, Winifred. *Playmaking with Children from Kindergarten to High School.* New York: Appleton-Century, 1957. A widely used text with an emphasis on storytelling.

Way, Brian. *Development through Drama.* New York: Humanities Press, 1972. Contains information regarding the relationship between child development and drama. Has many worthwhile activities.

PART II:

10 STEPS TO A SUPER PRODUCTION

STEP 1. *SELECTING THE PLAY*

So you're thinking about giving a play, have some concerns about your expertise, yet *know* you don't have time to peruse a lengthy volume on play production. Relax. We have answers, and a few secrets all bundled together to help you have a surefire hit. Best of all, the directions are concise and easily understood.

Modifying the Cast to Fit the Class or Group

This book contains adaptations of favorite fairy tales specifically written to give each student in an average-sized classroom a role. They can be given for or by children from the first grade up and are tailored to be short enough for all school functions.

The first play, *Cinderella* (p. 92), will be used as an example, so take a few minutes and read it. The suggestions are applicable to all plays.

The cast, as written, contains twenty-six people, thirteen boys and thirteen girls, eight of whom (those introduced at the ball) have no speaking parts. It can easily be modified to meet your needs. By combining roles and eliminating characters in the play, you can have a cast numbering anywhere between fourteen and thirty.

BOYS	GIRLS
1. Prince	Cinderella
2. King	Stepmother
3. Vendor/Merryweather	Marybella
4. Prime Minister	Isabella
5. Cook	Fairy Godmother

6. Page	Queen
7. Messenger	Princess
8. William/Mayberry	Dianna/Mistress Mayberry
9. George/Goldenhorn	Roseanne/Mistress Goldenhorn

CAN BE ELIMINATED:

10. Lord Goodenough	Lady Goodenough
11. Master Mayberry	Mistress Mayberry
12. Master Goldenhorn	Mistress Goldenhorn
13. Master Merryweather	Mistress Merryweather

William, George, and the vendor can also be cast as Masters Mayberry, Goldenhorn, and Merryweather. Dianna and Roseanne can become Mistresses Goldenhorn and Mayberry. This gives a cast of twenty-one. To make it smaller still, several roles can be combined. George and William, the page and the messenger, the prime minister and the cook, and Dianna and Roseanne can be played by four people instead of eight. Lord and Lady Goodenough can be eliminated. Now the cast is cut to fourteen—six boys and eight girls. (If this is done the people in Scene IV should be individually introduced.)

The cast can be easily enlarged, too. Obviously, more guests can be present at the ball. The lines of William and Dianna can be divided and played by four people. There can be two pages and a lady-in-waiting. The sexes of the minor characters can also be changed to meet your needs. William can become Wilhelmina, Dianna—Donald, and George—Georgette. It's simple and little or no rewriting is required.

Methods of Staging

If you're one of the fortunate few who has a revolving stage, innumerable flats, lots of battens, and plenty of wing and fly space, you've probably skipped over this part anyway. If not, and you're thinking, "OK, so the cast's no problem but how in the world am I going to manage six scenes?'', don't worry. Help is at hand!

Most schools, churches, recreational facilities, etc., have at least small stages in auditoriums or cafetoriums where a production can be presented. As is often the case, however, there is little room in the wings, the area on either side of the stage. The same is true of fly space, the space above the stage where backdrops, curtains, and other scenery may be hung from pipes or battens when not in use.

Our goal is to help you have an effective but simple presentation using the facilities that are available. In Step 5 you will be given more detailed instructions on designing the set, using flats, etc. In this section we will explain and discuss the three common methods of staging.

The most frequently used is the traditional proscenium type, which gets its name from the frame of the stage as it is seen from the audience. This is called the proscenium arch.

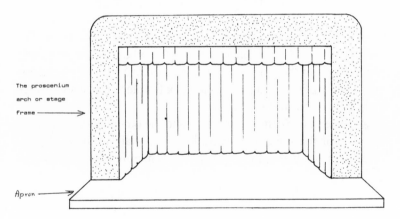

The stage as seen from the balcony.

The curved curtain or wall that is on the sides and back of the stage is called the cyclorama, or cyc for short. It and a few pieces of furniture are often all that are used for a set, which is the artificial setting of a scene.

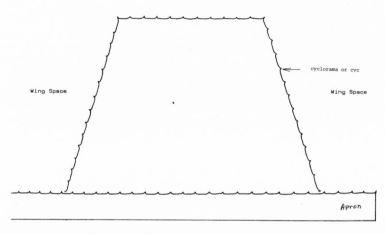

Floor plan of the stage with a cyc.

One way to stage *Cinderella* is to have the first scene, which takes place in the garden, played on the apron of the stage. This is the area in front of the main or act curtain. There should be no furniture in this section and the only props needed initially are some paper or plastic flowers, a hoe, and a flower basket. The curtain is closed, and Cinderella and the other characters simply walk out from the wings. Behind the curtain Scene II, with a few pieces of furniture and perhaps a mock fireplace, has been readied long before the start of the play.

At the end of Scene I Cinderella and the other characters exit at the side of the stage and go behind the curtain to their assigned places for the beginning of Scene II. When they are in position, pull the curtain.

After Scene II is finished the curtain closes and the royal family goes in front of the curtain to the apron of the stage to play Scene III. This takes place in a corridor in the palace. All actors stand during this time and there is no scenery. They exit at the side of the stage.

Meanwhile, behind the curtain, the furniture of Cinderella's house is quietly removed and two large chairs and two smaller ones are placed in the center of the stage for thrones.

After a brief pause, the curtain opens on Scene IV, the ball

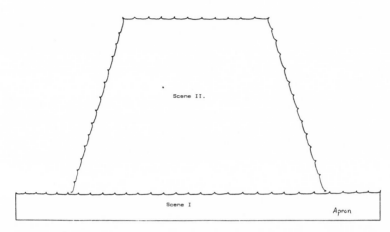

Staging plan.

room of the palace. On stage are the Prime Minister, the Messenger, the Page, and extras as desired. At the end of the scene the curtain is drawn, and, as before, Scene V is played in front of the curtain on the apron of the stage. While this is taking place the ballroom set is taken down, and the furniture which was on stage for Scene II, Cinderella's house, is put back in its original places.

When the curtain opens for Scene VI, Cinderella and her family are in their places on stage and the play proceeds until the final curtain.

Three-quarter or thrust staging is an optional method of presenting plays. Plays staged this way can be given in a cafeteria, gym, library, or any room large enough to accommodate a stage area and still have room for an audience. A platform may be used for the stage, but it is not necessary. There is no front curtain and changes of scene are indicated by turning off the stage lights. When using this type of staging, the audience sits on three sides of the acting area. Hinged screens or flats are used at the back and sides of the designated stage to hide the actors and props from those watching the play. Masking tape is often put on the floor to delineate the place where the action will occur.

If this type of staging is to be used, furniture should be kept to

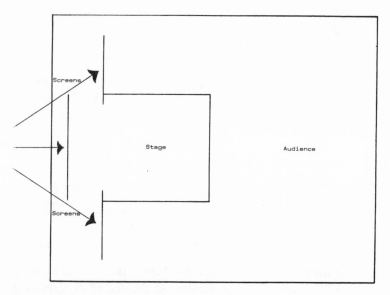

Floor plan for thrust staging.

a minimum. Scenes I, III, and V of Cinderella can be played on a blank stage very effectively, although artificial trees, benches, and columns can be used. The inside of the house could be only the suggestion of an interior, with perhaps three chairs; a bench and a chair, or a table, two straight chairs, and a rocker. A mantle front can suggest a fireplace. Scene changes should be carefully planned for all staging, with specific people selected to carry each item and put it in a designated location on or off stage. Scene changes should be rehearsed so they take less than two minutes. Keep the lights off and play background music during this time.

Thrust and theater-in-the-round stagings have several advantages over traditional methods and are effective, inexpensive methods of presentation. The proximity of the audience tends to create empathy. This makes spectators feel they are a part of the action. If the play is to be presented for children, they can be seated on the floor around the stage so that chairs for adults are all

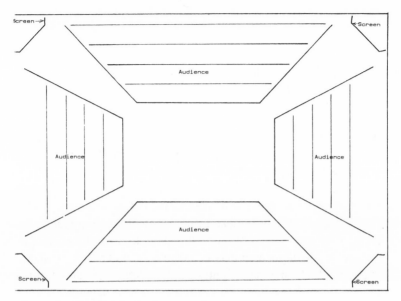

Floor plan for theater-in-the-round.

that are needed. It is also easy to tour in these ways, and this is great fun for a cast.

A play which is staged in-the-round has the audience seated on four sides with aisles going to the corners of the room. At the end of the aisles, screens are set up to mask the actors and props from the spectators. Dividing the cast into four groups instead of the traditional two or three can be advantageous because it is easier to keep children quiet offstage if they are fewer in number. Having adults with quiet games or books behind each screen is desirable for this reason. They can also help to see that entrances are made on time and actors don't peep out at the audience. All suggestions for three-quarter staging are also applicable for theater-in-the-round. The diagram below shows the layout for this type of staging. Step 2 will explain how to plan for a production staged in this manner.

STEP 2. *PLANNING THE PRODUCTION*

After you've decided on the play and the method of staging you're going to use, the next step is to prepare a prompt book which will contain all pertinent notes about the play to be produced.

A three-hole notebook with blank pages is essential. You can make copies of the plays in this book, and reduce and mount them. On the back of the sheet make a photocopy of the floor plan of the scene of the play that is opposite in the book. Smaller play scripts that cannot be duplicated may be taken apart and pasted on sheets of paper which have had slightly smaller rectangles cut out of the center. Two copies of the play will be needed if pages are not cut because one side of the play script will be placed face down on the larger sheet. This is done so there will be ample room for notes on movement, business, and other pertinent directing details.

Just what are movement and business? Movement is changing from one location to another on stage, as with the stepmother walking across the room and seating herself so that she can try on the glass slipper. Business is small movements of the hands, feet, or face, as when Cinderella takes the glass slipper out of her pocket and holds it up for the others to see. These should be planned in detail before the first rehearsal and noted in the margins of the prompt book so that wasted time is kept to a minimum. As you practice, some new ideas will probably occur to you. This is fine; however, try to keep changes to a minimum because they can be confusing to the actors.

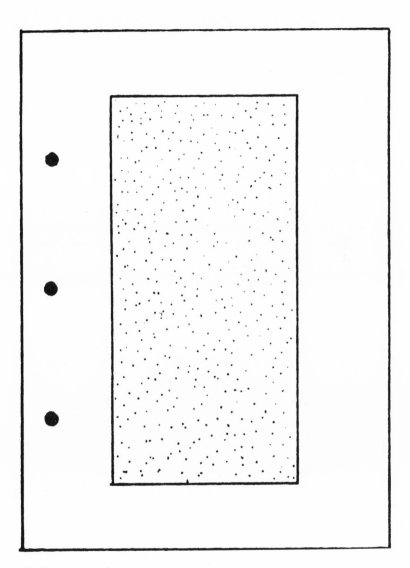

Binder page with center cut out.

Binder page with play script added.

In proscenium and thrust staging there are nine invisible areas of the stage, as shown in the drawing below.

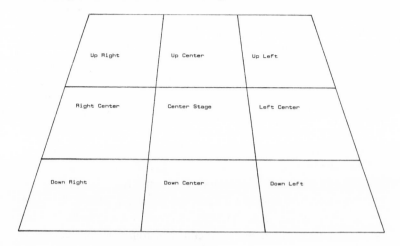

Up Right	Up Center	Up Left
Right Center	Center Stage	Left Center
Down Right	Down Center	Down Left

Floor plan showing areas of the stage.

Note that stage right side is on the actors' right as they face the audience. Stage left is to the left. The front of the stage is called downstage, and the back of the stage, or the parts furthest from the audience are called upstage. This is because at one time stages, instead of auditoriums, slanted. The area at the back was higher, so it was called upstage. You will need these terms in making descriptive notations in your prompt book and for giving directions to actors.

When the actors are told to move three steps forward, that means they are to move three steps in the direction they are facing. If they are squarely facing the audience when given that direction they should move downstage three steps. If backs are to the audience, they should move three steps upstage.

As a classroom exercise before starting rehearsals, it is fun to explain these things about the stage to the students and have them practice following directions. First, make a transparency of Diagram #7 and put it on the overhead projector. Show the areas on stage, then give directions such as "Move down center, stop, take three steps backwards,'' ''Cross up left, make a 90-degree turn to your right, then move forward two steps,'' etc.

Before starting to plan the action of the play, you should decide on the floor plan of the room or set where the action will take place, and make a scale drawing. The following is a workable plan for the interior of Cinderella's house, but there are many other acceptable ones. You should note that the furniture is placed so that it does not block entrances, and that the bench or small love seat is at an angle toward the front of the stage. This would seem strange in a home but looks normal on stage, and two actors may be seen when they are sitting on it conversing.

The next step is to read the scene several times, visualizing in your mind's eye where the actors will be on stage. Think of them as being in a picture with the actors representing a tableau. Consider groupings that are most pleasing and use these for the longest periods of time. Keep mental pictures in mind as you proceed to block out, or plan, the movement and business for the scene.

If this is your first play I suggest taking all the following steps, at least at the beginning. As you become more accustomed to directing, they will not be as necessary. Now you will need your prompt book, the scale drawings of the set, and buttons or pins with plastic heads to represent each actor on stage. Make lines on the drawing to show where exact movements are to be made. Keep the audience in mind to make sure that every spectator can see each actor on stage at any given moment. It's much easier than it sounds and will soon become second nature to you. The trick is to draw imaginary lines from the person on stage out into the auditorium. If one actor is standing in front of another from any angle, the person standing upstage is blocked. Actors should be taught that when this happens inadvertently during a performance, they should ''stage dress,'' which means move as inconspicuously as possible to a slightly different position where they can be seen by everyone.

When planning the action for the stage you should avoid all purposeless movement. You can, however, create reasons. For example, at the beginning of Scene II, Marybella is looking at herself in a hand mirror and saying, ''I feel exceptionally beautiful tonight.'' On the next line Isabella can walk to her, cross her arms

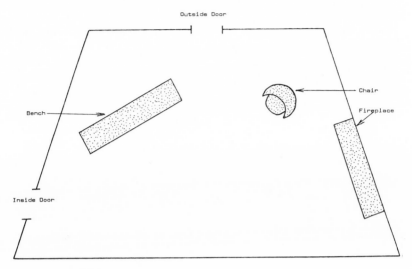

Floor plan of Cinderella's house.

This arrangement is boring because it is too symmetrical.
The stage as seen from the audience.

The stage as seen from the audience. An interesting arrangement of actors on stage.

while looking her over, then take the mirror and look at herself while saying, "Why, I'm much prettier than you and I have a wonderful personality, too."

This is where the fun of directing comes in, switching over to your right brain and letting the creativity flow. Just remember, actors don't wander aimlessly around the stage in a well-directed play. There is a reason for every movement, and actors generally talk when walking. There should be no fidgeting of hands or feet.

Keep areas of the stage in mind, too, because they can be used to advantage in achieving the effects you wish. Sections in the center of the stage are the strongest and are normally used by the actor who dominates the scene. Stage right is stronger than stage

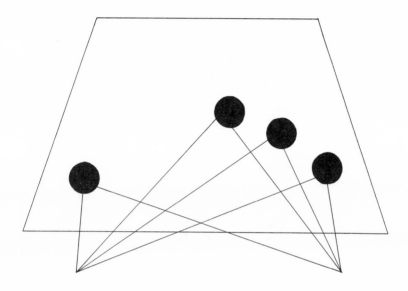

Arrangement showing actors in positions where they can be seen by everyone in the audience.

left because the audience, which reads from left to right, will tend to look there first. Upstage areas are preferable to downstage ones because they tend to become focal points, and because they force other actors to turn their heads to a profile or weaker position when they are conversing with anyone upstaging them.

If you are planning to present your play in-the-round this need not be considered because all areas are equally important. Instead you should plan the action to make sure that each actor faces every section of the audience at least once during a scene and that all parts of the stage are used.

It is also necessary to plan the "home" area for each actor. This insures that the number of people behind each screen is approximately the same the majority of the time. You will need to use this information when planning the entrances of the actors. We'll use *Cinderella* as the example. Screens are marked 1, 2, 3, and 4, and the characters are listed by their home bases. These are the areas from which initial entrances are made and where actors will be sitting most of the time when they are not in front of the audience.

In *Scene I,* Cinderella's garden, Entrance 3 represents the house. The other entrances are simply directions from which cast members arrive.

Scene II is inside Cinderella's home. Here Entrance 3 is used as a door going to other parts of the house. Entrance 1 is the outside

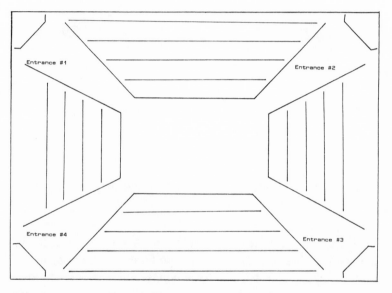

"Home entrances" for characters in *Cinderella.* Arena staging.

door. The stepmother, stepsisters, and Cinderella will all exit from this entrance during the scene because they are leaving the house and going to the ball.

In *Scene IV,* the ball scene, they will go on stage from Entrance 1 to be introduced by the Prime Minister. At the end of the scene they will return to their home screens, at Entrance 3. It is here they will make any clothing changes, such as removing the ball finery and Cinderella donning her rags. For this reason it is an all-girl entrance.

At the end of Scene V, which takes place outside the palace, Prince Raymond must exit through Entrance 1 in order to be able to enter through the front door of Cinderella's house during the last scene. All other actors enter and exit from their home areas.

Pre-planning the staging of a play before it goes into rehearsals has many advantages: 1) Time will not be wasted. 2) You will have a better-directed play because careful consideration has been given to every aspect of the production. 3) Actors will quickly become comfortable and confident in their roles and movements. 4) Your position as director will be immediately established and respected because you know exactly what you are doing and what you want to achieve.

STEP 3. *CASTING THE PLAY*

Deciding who is to be cast in each role should be the sole responsibility of the director, and there are many things to take into consideration. You should cast the major roles first and then fill in the minor ones with less talented or less experienced actors. Keep an open mind because very often you will be pleasantly surprised at how well some unappreciated student will do a part. That is why you should have tryouts for a play, rather than just appointing people for the roles.

Before tryouts select a few short scenes that will contain lines for all the characters in the play. This makes the actors feel their roles are important and will help to insure that a good performance is given by all. Explain the scene, have volunteers read first, and then select others you want to read.

Keep notes. Write down what you like and do not like, and who plays well together. Don't cast students in roles where they will be made to look ridiculous, such as a non-athletic girl in the role of star athlete or a homely boy as a handsome prince.

If you have difficulty deciding between two people, give them an imaginary situation and see how well they can improvise and stay in character. For example, tell the students to get into groups and plan a scene where Cinderella tries on one of her stepsister's dresses. Have the others make fun of her, and then let the stepmother tell her she can't go to the ball after all. This is a good way to locate the more creative pupils and also discover those who are natural at improvising and ad-libbing.

When deciding on the cast of a play, take into consideration those who have the most interest and enthusiasm because they will be more eager to practice and learn lines. Pay particular attention to the students who are not afraid to project enough to be heard in the room where the play is to be presented. Seeing actors moving their lips and having no idea what they are saying is terrible!

Good oral readers who have nice expression and timing are important, but don't stop here; you want the best. Consider height, appearance, physique, personality, leadership, dependability, intelligence, teamwork, and a record of cooperation. No announcement about the cast selection should be made until you are ready to name the role each person in the group will have.

STEP 4. *REHEARSING*

As with everything else, planning the rehearsals in advance makes a difference. The following is a schedule for *Cinderella*. It can be modified to be used for any of the plays in the book. Be sure to have a plan for each practice. Announce the days students are to be off books well in advance and make no exceptions. Prompt the actors who do not know their lines.

First Week—*Blocking Rehearsals.*

MON: Read the play and discuss it. Make corrections on oral interpretation, as needed.

TUES: Block out Scene I. (Tell cast movement and business.)

WED: Block out Scene II. Review Scene I.

THURS: Block out Scene III. Review Scene II.

FRI: Scenes I, II, III. Run-throughs.

Second Week—*Blocking Rehearsals.*

MON: Block out Scene IV. Review Scene III.

TUES: Block out Scene V. Review Scene IV.

WED: Block out Scene VI. Review Scene V.

THURS: Scenes I, II, III. Work on interpretation, movement, and business.

FRI: Scenes IV, V, VI. Work on interpretation, movement, and business.

Third Week—*Lines and details*

MON: Books off Scene I. *No* exceptions.

TUES: Practice lines Scene I. Movement and business details Scenes II and VI.

WED: Books off Scene II. *No* Exceptions. Review Scene VI.

THURS: Practice lines Scene II. Movement and business Scenes III and IV.

FRI: Books off Scene III. Movement and business Scene V.

Fourth Week—*Lines, details, and emphasis on picking up cues.*

MON: Practice lines Scene III. Review Scenes I and II.

TUES: Books off Scenes IV and V.

WED: Line practice Scenes IV and V. Details Scene VI.

THURS: Books off Scene VI.

FRI: Review Scene VI. Fast line practice all scenes at seats.

Fifth Week—*Polishing Rehearsals*

MON: Run through entire play for lines, movement, and business.

TUES: Work on key scenes that need polish.

WED: Rehearse entire play on stage. Use props and music. Give attention to lighting and technical details.

THURS: Videotape entire play on stage. No interruptions.

FRI: Play back videotape. Take notes. Discuss and critique.

Sixth Week—*Final Touches*

MON: Practice Curtain Call. Give individual coaching to special scenes and minor roles.

TUES: Run through entire play with all props, lights, sound effects, etc. No interruptions. Take notes and discuss them after rehearsals. Practice Curtain Call.

WED: Polishing rehearsal. Give attention to timing and details. *No interruptions.* After rehearsal give suggestions. Practice Curtain Call.

THURS: Dress rehearsal without makeup. Run this as a performance. Allow no interruptions. Give notes and suggestions afterward. Watch for dresses that are too long, colors that clash, clothes that don't fit well, etc.

FRI: Performance.

Plan on six weeks of rehearsals for each play. You will usually need to practice every scene the same number of times. Schedule at least six complete run-throughs with different areas of concentration. Students should be completely off books two weeks before performance. Allow time in the classroom for the students to practice their parts independently. You will be surprised at how much it helps even young children to practice lines this way, without your help. Beginning Wednesday of the fifth week eliminate the prompter; teach the actors that they are to learn their cues, the lines just before their own speech. If the person who is to give a cue forgets, the next actor gives that line, changing it a little if necessary, and then gives his or her own. This becomes easy with practice.

Make sure actors always stay in character. Do not *ever* allow anyone to whisper another person's line to him. This ruins the illusion you are trying to create. By training the actors to give each other's lines, there are no interruptions even if a line is forgotten and the play continues without anyone in the audience being aware that a mistake has been made. When actors are directed this way, a prompter is not needed during a performance, and you will have a polished production because the actors are "thinking on their feet."

When using proscenium staging, start training your actors from the first rehearsal to "open up." This means that their bodies face the audience, with head and eyes turned toward the actor who is speaking. Profile positions should generally be eliminated because they do not look natural on stage, an exception being two actors arguing nose-to-nose for humorous effect. By and large, the front of the body is much more interesting.

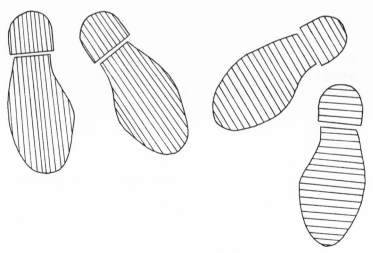

Feet placement for open positions.

Rules apply to stage stance as well. Feet should be flat on the floor and hands at sides, never in pockets unless called for. From the first rehearsal, students should start to know what is expected of them, including no unscheduled wandering about the stage.

Actors need to be taught to "stay in character," listen to what the others are saying, look at the one who is talking, and react to what is being said. Facial expressions and bodily movements are controlled at all times. Timing is essential, so devote some rehearsals to concentrating on "picking up cues." This means having actors say their lines immediately after the cue line has been given. These practices can be done sitting at desks or seated on the floor. Occasionally, see how fast lines can be given.

As you rehearse, have your students work to create the illusion of words being spoken for the first time. This means having lines sound natural, never memorized. Discussing the questions posed at the first rehearsal of the play will help.

You can add similar questions about each character in the cast to aid actors in getting the "feel" of their roles. They need to understand how characters think and why such statements are made. When actors have insight into the personalities of the persons they are portraying they can better interpret their roles and start becoming believable.

Body language is very important. Encourage your students to observe people the ages of the ones they are playing. Ask questions. For example: How would this person move? Would his shoulders be tense or relaxed? What kind of posture do you expect a king or a queen to have? Does a person look regal if his shoulders are slumped? Notice how older people use their arms to pull themselves up out of chairs. Does a sad person tend to walk fast or slowly? How would the character you are portraying walk?

Help the actors realize that they never relax on stage even though they appear to do so. The king must stay the king, with shoulders back and head up, even when he is not delivering lines. Hands and feet are a dead giveaway, too, if they are not controlled and still.

Modeling for inexperienced actors quickly shows them what to do. Watching a tape or movie and studying the voices, facial expressions, and movements of characters that are similar helps as well. When you see something that is good, stop the machine, rewind, explain what you are looking for, and then take a second look. (It's probably a good idea to play the tape in its entirety first, or you may have a disgruntled cast on your hands.)

Early in rehearsals start insisting that actors project. This means speaking loudly and clearly enough to be understood in every part of the auditorium. Projection is a matter of clarity and volume. While there has to be enough volume to carry to the back of the auditorium, it should never be confused with merely speaking loudly, and certainly not with yelling.

Even during the final rehearsals, when there are no interruptions, it is a good idea to sit at the back of the room and call ''Project!'' when needed in order to remind everyone to speak up. When videotaping be sure the camera is far enough away from the stage so it is difficult to hear anyone who is speaking softly. This will help more than anything you can say to teach the actors to speak loudly enough to be heard. Students love to watch themselves on tape and it is a wonderful way to improve and polish a production. Arrange to borrow a camera if the school does not have one.

Starting with the first rehearsal, insist that lines be given in a natural, convincing way. Once a ''sing-songy'' delivery has been established, it is almost impossible to eliminate. If this occurs, change the line slightly to get out of the awkward speech pattern, but keep the last few words the same to help the actor who has learned that cue for his next line. Remember, a production is only as good as its weakest actor, be he turnip or troubadour! Of course, you will spend more time polishing the major roles, but the most minor ones are also important and should not be neglected. One person can destroy the mood you and the cast have worked hard to create.

As director you need to make students realize that everything done on or off stage is important to the production. They should know that you expect them to do their best. A student who becomes uncooperative, doesn't learn lines on time, or follow the established rules, should be first reprimanded, then warned, then finally replaced. Stay in control; if you are firm, and hold your ground, students will soon learn that you will not tolerate unacceptable behavior, and discipline will not be a problem. Once you make a statement about policy, STICK with it. You will lose your credibility if you do not.

An actor who does not take the role seriously, deliver lines convincingly, or stay in character can ruin a play. Your job is to see that this doesn't happen. Start early to impress on each student just how important and necessary each part is to the production. If worse comes to worst, eliminate the role, let other actors say the lines, double cast, do ANYTHING to keep the offending student offstage. It simply is not fair to you or the students who have worked hard memorizing lines and rehearsing to have these efforts destroyed by some uncaring participant.

Keep all students busy offstage while you are conducting rehearsals. They can be doing the usual classroom assignments or special ones that are related to the production. For example, they can be designing programs, sets, costumes, or doing research projects on the period selected for the play. Have them writing character descriptions or practicing cues and lines with other students. This is also a a great time for doing creative writing. Suggestions for topics and discussions are given with each play, or you and your students may want to come up with some of your own.

The traditional method for staging a production is to have student crews help during rehearsals and while the production is taking place. This is a great way to get everyone involved, teach responsibility, and get yourself help. Naturally, the age of your students will make a difference, but even young children can do surprisingly well if they understand what is expected of them and have ample opportunity to practice.

A production staff might be composed of the following crews with one person in charge of each group.

Assistant director—your number one helper.

Production/Stage manager—responsible for seeing that rehearsals and performances run smoothly.

Prop Crew—assembles everything carried and used on stage. Makes sure it is available when needed.

House Crew—plans programs, ushering, and ticket sales.

Publicity—responsible for posters and news releases.

Costume Designers—plan the clothing worn on stage.

Makeup Crews—do the actors' makeup.

Carpenters—build sets.

Light and Sound Crews—responsible for lights and sound.

Set Designers—design the sets.

Paint Crew—paints sets and props.

Be sure to recognize the contributions of crew members by putting every name on the program.

During the last two weeks of rehearsals all props, music, lights, and sound cues should be used. This is important for the actors on stage and those in the wings who are acting as the stage crew. Teach the crews to check all props to see that they are in their proper places, to make scene changes rapidly, and to have light and sound cues smooth. Tape all music to be played between the scenes and any sound effects from records (especially ordered from catalogs or shops). These can be played back perfectly cued when you use a machine with a tape counter. A room sound system can be most effective if one is available.

Devote time to technical rehearsals for the stage, lights, and prop crews. They can ruin a play if they do not know exactly what to do.

STEP 5. *THE SET*

Proscenium staging is ideally done with flats, or wooden frames, covered with strong cotton canvas, masonite, or quarter-inch plywood. The latter are less expensive, but they are heavy. Flats are typically four feet by eight feet, but dimensions vary as needed. On stage they are lashed together at the back with ropes or hinged with loose-pin hinges that can be rapidly removed. A well-stocked theater will have numerous plain flats and additional door and window flats of various types. They can be repeatedly repainted, put in any order, and used to create entirely different backgrounds. One set can be in the wings or flown—raised above the stage—while another set or backdrop is being used.

The usual procedure for designing a set is to first draw sketches to see how the stage would look from the audience. Second, make a scaled floor plan of the stage showing how to place the flats. This will enable you to know if you have an adequate number of flats or if you need to build more. If you are working with more advanced students, you can have them design sets as individuals or work as teams.

Students can also make scaled elevated drawings of the front of the set and actual construction drawings of the back. These are the type that can be used in shop classes for building the flats. Model sets can also be made, the accuracy depending on the level of the students. They are fun for all concerned.

Even if you've never been backstage in a theater you're probably familiar with the backdrop curtains used on stage and shown in movies. These are large, flat curtains that are hung at the back of the stage. They usually have a pipe or chain in the hem to ensure they're hanging straight. Scenes are painted on these

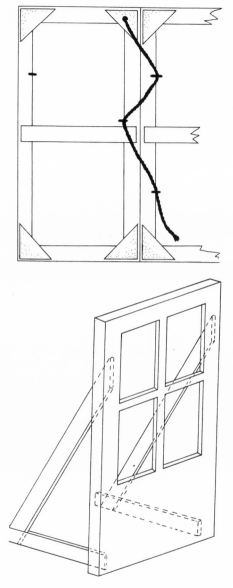

Top. Theatrical flat constructed of 1″ × 4″ pine lumber. Notice lash line used to hold two flats in place.
Bottom. Window flat showing back bracing.

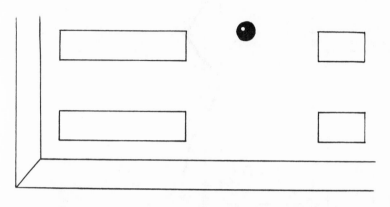

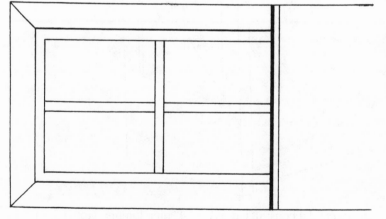

Window and door flats as seen from the audience.

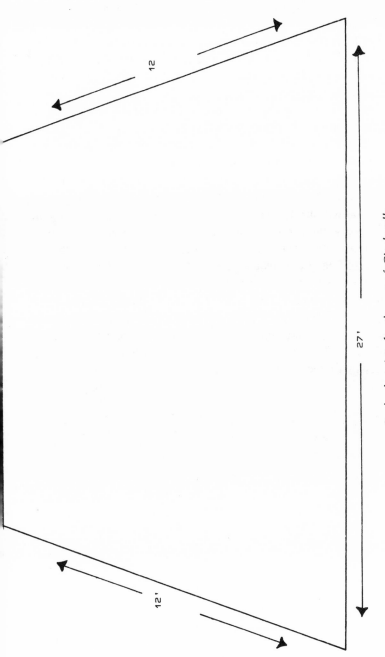

Scale drawing for the set of *Cinderella*.

drops, and although unrealistic unless expertly done, they can be very effective.

Let's say that you have a window in the interior of Cinderella's house not far from the front door. An exterior scene could be painted on the drop behind it, and actors would then be visible through the window as they approach the front door. This would be quite effective in the last scene of *Cinderella* when the pages, prime minister, and prince come to the house.

If it is not feasible to have elaborate staging such as the ones mentioned here, do not be concerned. The plays included in this book can be staged effectively with a simple cyc, the curtains around the stage, or simpler still, in the round. If this method is used you will need screens to mask the actors and props from the audience. Again, commercial screens or hinged flats are certainly preferable, but there are other alternatives. It is possible to purchase heavy corrugated cardboard or open large refrigerator boxes to make screens for backgrounds. These can then be taped together and painted. This is inexpensive, but even paint and glue are not free, so there are costs involved and there are far superior methods. If you are forced to use cardboard screens, store them flat on the floor if they are not framed. If this is not done your screens will become warped and bent.

STEP 6. *PROPS*

Properties, or props, are anything used on stage that are not sets. Hand props, as the name suggests, are items which can be carried. They are usually part of the business of the play and include such things as glasses, brooms, books, flowers, etc.

Early in rehearsal, as a class assignment, have the students read through each scene in the play and make lists of all properties that are to be used. Next, list the props by entrances. Let's say you've decided to use arena staging, have blocked out the play, and know the home bases for your actors as shown on pages 50, 68–70. Now, as you read through the list of props, think of the person who will be using each one or carrying it on stage. Make a note of the entrance that will be used and place the prop behind that screen. It is well worth the time it takes to make a master diagram showing the scene, people, and props coming from an entrance. This is how it's done:

ARENA STAGING PROP LIST FOR *CINDERELLA*

Entrance 1	Entrance 2	Entrance 3	Entrance 4
Messenger's scroll	four thrones	flowers	bucket
bugle		flower basket	scrub brush
glass slipper		hoe	bench
		broom	chair
		wand	fireplace
		mousetrap/mice	
		fan	
		shawl	
		face powder	
		puff	
		glass slipper	
		sewing basket	
		needle	
		thread	
		scissors	
		pin cushion	
		sewing	

PROP AND PEOPLE PLAN FOR *CINDERELLA*

Scene 1—Cinderella's Garden

Entrance 1	Entrance 2	Entrance 3	Entrance 4
Enter during scene:	Enter during scene:	Enter during scene:	Enter during scene:
Dianna with money	*William* with money	*Cinderella* flowers flower basket	*Vendor* fruit box fruit bell
Messenger with scroll		*Stepmother* broom	*George* money
Page, with bugle and banner		*Marybella*	
		Isabella	

Scene 2—Cinderella's House

Entrance 1	Entrance 2	Entrance 3	Entrance 4
		On stage:	*Place furniture on stage for Cinderella's house before start of scene
		Cinderella, sewing basket needle thread scissors	
			*Remove furniture after scene
		Marybella mirror	
		Isabella	
		Stepmother watch fan shawl face powder puff bag	
		Godmother wand mousetrap	

Scene 3—The Palace

Entrance 1	Entrance 2	Entrance 3	Entrance 4
	On stage at opening:		
	King		
	Queen		
	Princess		
	Prince		
	Enter during scene:		
	Cook		

Scene 4—The Ball

Entrance 1	Entrance 2	Entrance 3	Entrance 4
On stage at opening:	On stage at opening:		Enter during scene:
Prime Minister	*four thrones		*Lord Goodenough*
Messenger	Enter during scene:		*Lady Goodenough*
Page	*King*		*Mr. Goldenhorn*
Enter during scene:	*Queen*		*Ms. Goldenhorn*
Mr. Merryweather	*Prince*		
Ms. Merryweather	*Princess*		
Stepmother	*Remove thrones at end of scene		
Marybella			
Isabella			
Cinderella			

Scene 5—A Terrace at the Palace

Entrance 1	Entrance 2	Entrance 3	Entrance 4
Chimes ring during scene		On stage at opening: *Prince*	On stage at opening: *Cinderella*
		Prince watch	
		(He exits #1)	

Scene 6—Cinderella's House

Entrance 1	Entrance 2	Entrance 3	Entrance 4
Enter during scene:		On stage at opening:	On stage at opening:
Prime Minister		*Cinderella* sewing basket	chair bench
Page		needle thread	fireplace scrub brush
Messenger			brush
		Stepmother	
Roseanne			
		Isabella	
Prince			

Start working with props early in rehearsals so that actors are comfortable using them. Some props can be art projects. Painted fruit made out of papier-mâché and crepe paper flowers are examples. By using your imagination, you will be able to come up with many more items that students will enjoy preparing. The page's bugle can be a plumber's plunger sprayed gold. A fringed banner hanging from it adds just the right touch. Plastic mugs and goblets can be painted in the same manner, though students should pantomime eating and drinking on stage because of the danger of choking. Parents and grandparents (lots of attics and old trunks with memorabilia) can be great resources. Make prop lists early and send them home with your students. Don't be afraid to ask for help. It's so much easier if you do. Often people really want to be of assistance but they're hesitant to make the first move. Make it easy for them.

STEP 7. *COSTUMES*

In professional productions there is a costume designer who does research on the period in which the play is set. Clothing is then designed to be appropriate for the selected time period. Care is taken to make it of a type that is in keeping with the personality of the character being portrayed. Fabrics and colors are planned and coordinated. The stars are often given warmer, brighter colors (reds, oranges, yellows) than those worn by the actors with supporting roles. This automatically enables them to command more attention on stage.

If you are artistic, you'll enjoy designing the costumes for the play. If not, recruit a talented friend, parent, or older student to help. This is a great project. With each play in the book, under the section for enrichment activities, you will find suggested periods and countries where clothing is particularly interesting or easy to acquire.

A typical way of securing costumes involves looking in attics, closets, thrift shops, flea markets, and garage sales and discovering something that can be combined with another article to make it satisfactory. Little girls who have been flower girls in weddings or who study dancing often have costumes that are quite workable. Occasionally, one worn for Halloween may be used. Costume rental shops are another possibility but they are expensive. Do not use paper costumes. They are unrealistic, tear easily, and can be more expensive than costumes made by combining available clothing.

A woman's full skirt and matching blouse can become a floor-length dress for a young girl by adding a tuck or two and putting some safety pins to good use. Of course, evening dresses that are altered to fit can make lovely ball gowns. Satins and velvets reflect light in such ways as to suggest opulence. Taffeta, brocades, sequined, and metallic clothing can also be extremely effective.

Baseball pants and long socks are readily available and can be a blessing for the boys. Worn with an adult-size turtleneck shirt and belted, you have very presentable attire. If you are using girls to play the parts of boys, as the dwarfs in Snow White, get matching tights and overblouses, add a belt, perhaps some colored shorts, and you have a great outfit! A man's smoking jacket can become a regal robe for a young king. Flashy costume jewelry is wonderful for royalty. Glitter glues are also an inexpensive way to dress up an outfit. A word of caution: be careful about shoes. Check on these early. A pair of sneakers can completely destroy the effect you are trying to achieve. If necessary, cover them with a pair of men's black socks which have had the tops cut off so they can fold inside the gym shoes. Add a gilded cardboard buckle and you have something closely resembling a pair of period shoes.

Be sure to request that all costumes be brought in early to see that colors blend, clothing is satisfactory, and you don't have all pink dresses! Contrasts and variety are interesting. Schedule a dress rehearsal to make sure that the girls don't trip on dresses that are too long or wear skirts that are too short. Comic characters, such as the stepmother and stepsisters, can wear exaggerated costumes to help make their parts more humorous. Have a supply of safety pins of all sizes, needles, several shades of thread, and wide masking tape, which in an emergency can be used to tape up hems and hold together costumes. Take extra skirts, shirts, sashes, belts, and jewelry. You never know what may just be the right touch. With a little foresight and planning, you'll be prepared for those unexpected events, which, of course, are going to occur!

STEP 8. *MAKEUP*

Greasepaint is used for productions in large auditoriums under strong theatrical lights. In intimate theater, and in plays with young children, a woman's base makeup is usually used. This makes girls feel glamourous and grown up, but it should be used sparingly. Boys' makeup should be slightly darker and made to look as natural as possible. Never use lipstick with them; put brown eyeliner on lips and eyebrows instead. Be careful about applying makeup to eyelids. Sometimes the skin there is very fragile and you may find yourself with a handful of blood.

Inexperienced people are often tempted to produce overly rouged, kewpie-doll effects which look ridiculous. Explain what you want to achieve before anyone starts putting on makeup. That way you're less likely to have to remove someone's creative endeavors.

If you are working with elementary-age children, it's better to gray hair, add a line or two, and forget it. They don't like to sit still long enough for a makeup job, and their skins are so young it's almost impossible to age them realistically. By middle-school and junior-high ages you can actually start getting into realistic makeup.

To convincingly age a person, a light makeup base is used first, and then a darker makeup or eye shadow is put over the indented parts of the face. These are the areas above the eyes, under the cheeks, in the temples, in the cleft of the chin, and on the section that extends from the corners of the nose to the mouth. What you are actually doing is molding a face. Next, you should start to paint a new one on top of what you have just created. Have young, unlined actors smile and frown so that you can discover where lines will eventually be. Next draw them in at the corners of the eyes, between the eyebrows, on the forehead, from the sides of the nose to the mouth, and in the center of the chin.

These areas have already been darkened with the liner, and now you're going to need a rachel or white outline stick between the lines to highlight them. For every dark line there should be a light one in order to create the illusion of wrinkles. Makeup should be powdered after application to keep it from smearing. Cold cream and soap and water will remove it.

Students love demonstrations of how to apply makeup for a fantasy world. Show them so they get the idea, then let them practice with pencil and paper. Start with two identical faces and have them age one using the techniques just discussed. First shade or mold the face, add the lines, then erase between lines for highlights. They'll be amazed at the difference in the two faces, and it's a great art lesson!

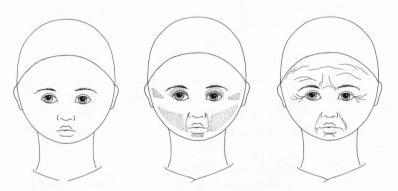

Left: Picture of a child without makeup. *Center:* The dotted areas indicate where darker makeup should be added in order to mold the face. *Right:* Illustration showing where lines should be added to age a person.

With practice you can learn to make sideburns, mustaches and beards look completely natural. This is done with crepe hair which can be ordered from play catalogs if not readily available. First iron the hair so it will straighten and then cut it into lengths approximately the size that will be needed. For sideburns and mustaches, which will be applied in layers, this is usually about half an inch. Paint the area where hair is to be applied with spirit gum and wait for it to become tacky. Hair put on before this will not stick. Smooth the crepe hair so that it is the same thickness throughout and put it on the skin. Press the hair with scissors a few seconds until the adhesive dries. Continue to apply small amounts of hair until the effect is realistic. Trim as needed. Apply an extra layer of spirit gum, and the crepe hair will stay until removed with spirit gum remover or cold cream.

Hair color can be changed with colored hair sprays. It may be greyed or whitened with cornstarch, white powder, or even white shoe polish. Nose putty can be used to change the size and shape of this feature and for making scars and warts. An eyebrow pencil can do a great deal to help you achieve the effect you want, although it is not the true realism you see in the movies and on TV. You will find several books listed in the bibliography which go into more detail on makeup.

STEP 9. *LIGHTING*

Professional production companies spend large amounts of money on lighting equipment. We'll discuss this briefly, but chances are you are a third grade teacher who has been told you are responsible for a PTA program or an assembly, and you're much more interested in knowing how to use what you have effectively.

If you have a dimmer board or remote control color wheel in front of your spot and floodlights, marvelous special effects can be achieved. Light, unobtrusive because it is silent, can be used to cast an almost magical spell that subtly affects the emotions. For example, in a tragedy or suspense play, lights can be gradually faded from warm to cool or white colors. This creates a feeling of foreboding or impending disaster without anyone in the audience knowing why.

Plain, uncolored bulbs such as the ones used in home lighting are most ineffective on stage because they produce flat, uninteresting effects. The use of colored lights surprisingly makes everything appear natural. The three colors of light which are called light primaries are red, green, and blue. When they are blended together they give the sensation of being white. Adding some straw or amber lights can help to create a sparkle and brilliance in costumes. Most theatrical equipment comes with mounting brackets for gels. These are colored plastic, vinyl, or glass sheets which may be inserted to change the color of lights.

Take care to achieve a balance of color. The use of complimentary colors, such as red lights on a green dress, will give the audience the illusion of seeing a black one. Green light on a red dress will do the same. In general, warm colors, variations of reds and ambers, are more predominately used in comedies and fantasies. Cool colors, such as various blues and greens, are used more often in serious dramas and mysteries.

Spotlights are effective when mounted from what would be the front of a first balcony. They are focused in such a way as to give equal lighting to all areas of the stage. Warmer colors are usually placed on one side of the auditorium and cooler colors on the other. Footlights and lights hung from a batten at the top of the stage should be supplemented with other lights because they give the poorest type of illumination for stage. Hold a flashlight directly above and below your face and you will get the idea. If

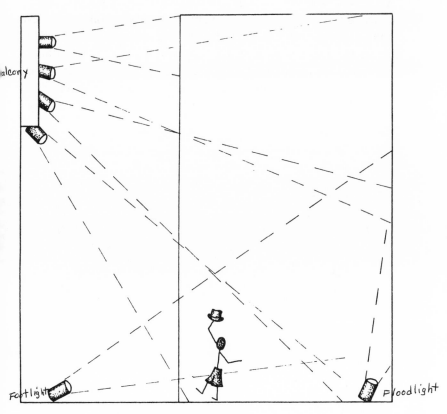

Light placement for proscenium staging.

that's all that's available, you are certainly not alone. Adding two spotlights on either side of the stage or audience will improve lighting a great deal. They should be mounted so that the beams of lights cross.

Spotlights and floodlights can be made from one-gallon tin cans with porcelain sockets wired to the bottoms for floodlights. Household dimmers of proper wattage may be attached. Students from the sixth grade up may make them as a science project, and they are fairly effective.

For theater-in-the-round spotlights should be placed on all sides of the room and focused so that they cross each other. As with every aspect of staging, specially scheduled rehearsals which concentrate on lighting will help polish the production. In proscenium staging, turn the lights on the front curtain immediately before the scene is to start; this is called teasing. Even without elaborate equipment you can create some special effects. For example, when the fairy godmother in *Cinderella* waves her wand, have the lights flash on and off to show that something very

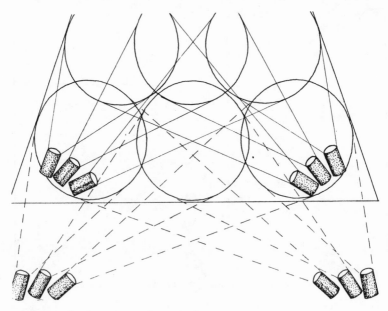

Lighting plot for proscenium staging.

unusual is happening. Use your imagination and you will find other ways to make lights work for you. Again, the bibliography has a list of good books which are more detailed.

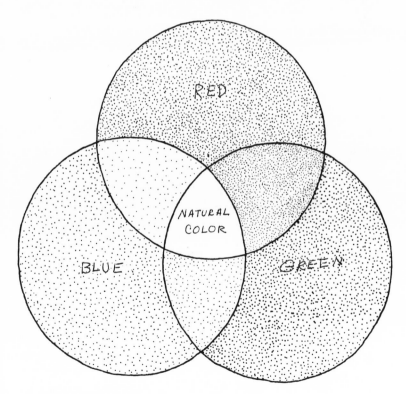

Color wheel for lights.

STEP 10. *PERFORMANCE DAY CHECKLIST*

So performance day has finally arrived! You will hopefully be giving more than one. Rest homes, senior citizen centers, and retirement communities are usually delighted to have presentations. Giving your play for them first is an excellent way to polish a performance. Besides, it's fun, and everyone loves the good feeling that comes from bringing pleasure to others.

Regardless of where you give your play, the production should be so well planned and organized backstage that you are no longer needed and can take a seat in the audience to enjoy watching what you have created. This also gives the advantage of having the authority figure watching the performance. The occasional students who might think it's funny to disregard directions will be much less tempted if they know you are watching!

Have a checklist of things you, or someone you trust, must do on this special day. It might include some of the following items:

1. Make sure that the student-designed programs are in their proper places. They are usually given out by students on the house crew.
2. Select an adult to be responsible for having the program people at their stations at the proper time.
3. See that all props are in place on and off stage.
4. If chairs are to be set up, make sure they are properly placed.
5. Alert a few responsible people in the audience to the fact that aisles must not be blocked for theatre-in-the-round. Marking them with masking tape will help.
6. Check makeup and costumes to make sure everything is satisfactory.

7. See that copies of the master plan for props and people, (pages 68–70) and copies of the play are near all entrances.
8. Talk to the people in charge of sound-effects tapes and the background music. They need to check out equipment and cue tapes.
9. Remind the light-crew head that all lights need to be working properly. Burned-out bulbs need to be replaced.
10. Check to see that the person responsible for videotaping the performance has a new tape and knows the best place to be when recording.
11. Go over the following points with your students before curtain time:
    • Make sure they understand that they are to be hidden from the audience until seen on stage.
    • Warn them again that there is to be no peeping around, under, or at the sides of the curtains or screens.
    • Remind them that they are to be absolutely quiet offstage because even whispers carry to the audience. Extraneous noise can ruin the performance that you have all worked so hard to achieve.
    • Tell the students of your expectations of them: a polished performance with all actors projecting, reacting, and doing just what you've been practicing.
    • Remind them that by their working together to help each other, they can give a play that will make everyone pleased and proud.
12. Make sure that the play starts exactly on time. A touch of class!
13. Smile. Relax and know that your careful planning is going to help your cast and crews have a super production. Because of it everyone involved will have memories filled with the pride that comes from knowing they've done their very best.

BIBLIOGRAPHY FOR PART II

This section of the bibliography contains references to resource materials that will be helpful for producing a play.

Albala, Leila. *Easy Halloween Costumes for Children.* Chambly, Quebec, Canada: Alpel, 1986, 2nd revised edition. An excellent, easy-to-understand book that has miniature patterns of costumes and accessories which can be enlarged to fit anyone.

Allensworth, Carl. *The Complete Play Production Handbook.* New York: Harper & Row, 1982. This book is all-inclusive. It has particularly good sections on musicals, sound effects, dialogue, and building a scene.

Barton, Lucy. *Historic Costumes for the Stage.* Boston: Walter H. Baker, 1935. This book is a classic. It covers a wide range of periods and contains much information on costumes and accessories.

Buckman, Herman. *Stage Make-up.* New York: Watson-Guptill Publications, 1971. Step-by-step instructions for all types of makeup are included in this text. Directions and illustrations are clear, concise, and easy to understand.

Chilver, Peter. *Staging a School Play.* New York: Harper & Row, 1967. Teachers/directors will find help in casting, crewing, setting up, and other aspects of production.

Corson, Richard. *Stage Make-up.* Englewood Cliffs, NJ: Prentice Hall, 1981, revised. This is another classic. It has everything you've always wanted to know about theatrical makeup.

Cummins, Richard. *101 Costumes for All Occasions.* Boston: Plays, Inc., 1987. Cummins' book is packed with suggestions for easy, inexpensive costumes.

Dean, Alexander, and Lawrence Carra. *Fundamentals of Play Directing.* New York: Holt, Rinehart and Winston, 1974. Polishing procedures and ways of getting the most out of a production. For the advanced director.

Dolman, John, revised by Richard Korauf. *The Art of Play Production.* New York: Harper & Row, 1973. A college textbook containing all aspects of production, acting, and directing.

Engler, Larry, and Carol Fijun. *Making Puppets Come Alive.* New York: Taplinger Publishing Co., 1973. This book deals with the manipulation of puppets and includes all basic movements. Photographs are excellent.

Flower, Cedric, and Alan Jon Fortney. *Puppets.* Worcester, MA: Davis Publications, 1983. Helpful instructions are given for making various types of puppets and marionettes.

Fredericks, Mary, with Joyce Segal. *Creative Puppetry in the Class-room.* Rowayton, CT: New Plays, 1979. All facets of puppetry are covered: activities, props, scenes, and the making and using of puppets.

Hake, Herbert V. *Here's How.* Evanston, IL: Row, Peterson, and Company, 1968. Hake's book is so clearly written and illustrated that anyone can understand the principles of lighting and stagecraft in a few minutes. Better still, the emphasis is on economy as well.

Harrold, Robert, and Phillipa Legg. *Folk Costumes of the World.* New York: Sterling Publishing Co., 1981. The dramaturgists in your classroom will enjoy doing research using this book on costumes.

Hoggett, Chris. *Stage Crafts.* New York: St. Martin's Press, 1975. This book is an excellent source of information on all aspects of scenery construction and lightning.

Legat, Michael. *Putting on a Play.* New York: St. Martin's Press, 1984. This guide to theater production is comprehensive and practical. It is particularly valuable because it is pertinent to amateur productions.

Lounsburg, Warren C. *A Concise Encyclopedia of Stagecraft from Alternating Current to Zoom Lens: Theatre Backstage from A to Z.* Seattle and London: University of Washington Press, 1967. As the title states, answers to staging questions are easily found in this well-done volume.

Murray, W. Lynn. *Handbook for One-Act Play Directors, Critic Judges and Contest Managers.* Austin, TX: The University Interscholastic League, 1988, 11th edition. Written primarily for interscholastic league participants, this little book contains a wealth of information on directing and staging. In addition, there is a comprehensive anthology of approved one-act plays.

River, Elsie, and Margaret Sharp. *Guiding Children.* Nashville, TN: Convention Press. This book has numerous art, dramatic, and research projects which can easily be adapted for enrichment activities when presenting a play.

Rudin, Helen. *The Story of Clothes.* New York: Playmore Inc. and Waldman Publishing Corp., 1984. You can find this book at supermarkets for less than $1.00 and it contains lots of good information on clothing through the ages. In addition there are interesting art activities related to costume designing.

Sellman, Hunton, and Merrill Lessley. *Essentials of Stage Lighting.* Englewood Cliffs, NJ: Prentice-Hall, 1982. You'll find the answers to all your questions on lighting equipment, and how to achieve the effects you want.

Smith, Dick. *Do-It-Yourself Monster Make-up.* New York: Harmony Books, 1986. Your students will really enjoy studying the illustrations and practicing doing monster makeups. It's a fun way to increase makeup expertise.

Spanabel, Emery, Jay. *Stage Costume Techniques.* Englewood Cliffs, NJ: Prentice-Hall, 1981. This book deals with designer responsibility, costume coordination, alterations, fabrics, and basic clothing construction.

Williams, John T. *Costumes and Settings for Shakespeare's Plays.* Totowa, NJ: Barnes and Noble Books, 1982. This book has good illustrations and information on the clothing of the period.

Wilson, Edwin. *The Theatre Experience.* New York: McGraw-Hill, 1980. A teacher/director should find this book dealing with staging and directing very helpful.

PART III:

LARGE-CAST PLAYS

GETTING STARTED

The plays in this book differ from those in other collections in two ways. First, they may be legally reproduced. Second, you are encouraged to adapt them to your needs. If a line is awkward for a student, change it; just keep the cue the same. If you need a different size cast, follow the suggestions for modifying it to your specifications.

Before each play you will find topics for discussion, creative writing, and reports. Also included are activities for projects which may be done by students working individually or in groups. Each play is set in a different country. This provides excellent motivation for the pupils becoming more knowledgeable about the locale. Specific dates are given for several plays. This is because there was an interaction between that country and the United States during the period. Enrichment activities are often a natural outgrowth of what transpired. The illustrations that follow show some of the projects that may be done in conjunction with studying or presenting the play.

Box scene.

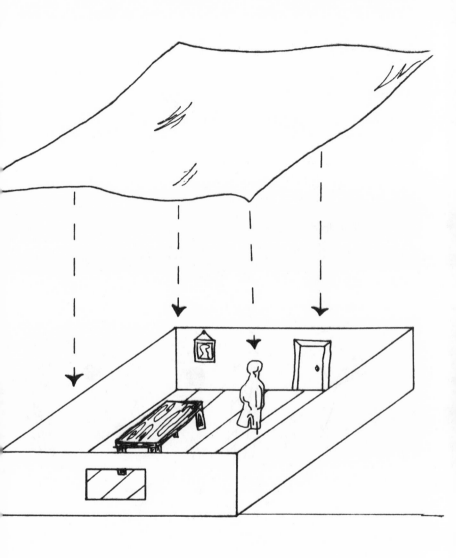

Peep box.

Accordion-fold pictures.

Coat-hanger puppet.

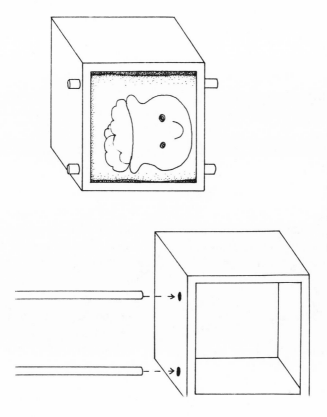

Television box.

CINDERELLA

Cast of Characters

William, Cinderella's friend
Vendor, a fruit salesman
George, a neighbor
Prince

The King

Cook, the king's chef
Prime Minister
Lord Goodenough, a guest
Master Mayberry, a guest
Master Goldenhorn, a guest
Master Merryweather, a guest
Messenger, a herald
Page, the king's attendant

Cinderella, an orphan girl
Stepmother, a mean lady
Dianna, Cinderella's friend
Isabella, Cinderella's
  stepsister
Marybella, Cinderella's
  stepsister
Godmother, a good fairy
The Queen
The Princess
Mistress Mayberry, a guest
Mistress Goldenhorn, a guest
Lady Goodenough, a guest
Roseanne, a neighbor

Production Notes

Production notes for Cinderella are given in the section entitled *10 Steps to a Super Production* (pages 35–40, 46–56, 66–70).

Discussion Questions

The following may be used as a basis for topics for creative writing or for discussion questions:

1. Cinderella seemed to think that if she and her sisters married wealthy men they would have happy lives. Do you think this is true? Why, or why not?

2. Is marriage a solution to life's problems? Do people ever live happily ever after?

3. In many fairy tales there is a wicked stepmother. Are all stepparents evil? Write a story about a good stepparent.

4. Why do you think Cinderella's stepmother and stepsisters were so mean to her?

5. Why did Cinderella continue to live with them? At the time the play is set it was difficult for a young woman to support herself. How can girls prepare themselves now to live independently?

6. Cinderella's family was very unkind to her. Have you ever had anyone treat you badly? How did it make you feel? What did you do about it?

7. Write a story about a boy or girl who is badly treated.

8. The Prince and Cinderella knew each other for only a short time before they decided to get married. Does this happen in real life? Why is this desirable/undesirable?

9. Cinderella could not talk to anyone about her problems. It is different today. If young people are given abusive treatment what can they do? Where can they go for help?

10. The Prince was going to take Cinderella away from the miserable life she had been leading. Realistically, what were her

chances of having this happen? What other methods of escape did she have?

Enrichment Activities

Suggestions for the teacher For research purposes set the play in Italy. Have students do an activity from at least one category and teach the class what they have learned. Assignments may be done by students working individually or in groups.

Select one of the following projects to do:

1. Make a poster showing Roman numerals from 1 to 1,000.
2. Make a model of an ancient Roman building.
3. Make a model of the room in Cinderella's home that is used for Scenes II and VI. Decorate it the way you think Cinderella's stepmother would have decorated it.
4. Make a model of the room described in #3. Decorate it the way you think Cinderella would have decorated it.
5. Make puppets of the characters in Cinderella.
6. Illustrate the clothing worn by ancient Romans and traditional Italian costumes.
7. Make a relief map of Italy.

Write a report on one of the following:

1. Italy. Tell about the climate, principal crops, major exports, cities, and recreation.
2. Romulus and Remus
3. Julius Caesar
4. Leonardo da Vinci
5. Venice
6. Italian foods
7. The Colosseum in Rome
8. The Leaning Tower of Pisa
9. Recreation in Italy
10. The Roman Empire
11. Ancient Rome

Cinderella—Play Script

SCENE I. Cinderella's garden.

   As the scene opens Cinderella is weeding her flowers. William enters.

WILLIAM: Good morning, Cinderella.

CINDERELLA: Why, good morning, William.

WILLIAM: You seem to be working hard.

CINDERELLA: Yes, but I like to be outside where it's so peaceful.

WILLIAM: I do, too. That's why I take walks every day.

CINDERELLA: I'm sure you enjoy that.

WILLIAM: I certainly do. I like getting to talk to you, too, even though you never stop working.

CINDERELLA: I really can't, there's just too much to be done.

WILLIAM: You do a fine job on your garden. These flowers are mighty pretty.

CINDERELLA: Thank you.

WILLIAM: (*Picking a flower and smelling it*) Smells good, too.

CINDERELLA: I think so. But they wouldn't for long if I didn't keep after these weeds.

STEPMOTHER: (*Entering*) Cinderella, quit that talking and get to work!

CINDERELLA: Yes, Stepmother.

STEPMOTHER: (*To William*) And you. You have no business being here picking my flowers.

WILLIAM: Just one.

STEPMOTHER: You leave this minute, or I'll have you arrested.

WILLIAM: All right. I'm leaving. (*Starting off stage*)

STEPMOTHER: And don't come back.

WILLIAM: Who wants to?

CINDERELLA: I'm sorry, William. (*Stepmother gives her a dirty look.*)

STEPMOTHER: Anyone else would have been through long ago.

CINDERELLA: Yes, Ma'am.

STEPMOTHER: Well, let's work a little faster. (*She exits*)

CINDERELLA: I'll try, Stepmother.

(*Cinderella continues working. Dianna enters.*)

DIANNA: Hi, Cinderella.

CINDERELLA: Hello, Dianna. Nice to see you.

DIANNA: You too. Say, there's a big fair in town and I want you to go with me.

CINDERELLA: Oh, but I couldn't.

DIANNA: Why not? Won't your stepmother let you?

CINDERELLA: No. There's so much to do. I never get through with my work until late at night.

DIANNA: Don't you ever get to have any fun? (*Cinderella shakes her head sadly.*)

STEPMOTHER: Cinderella, I caught you talking again. You're going to be punished.

DIANNA: But she was working all the time.

STEPMOTHER: (*To Dianna*) That's no business of yours. Cinderella, you've been disobeying. There'll be no supper for you tonight.

CINDERELLA: Yes, Ma'am.

STEPMOTHER: Now you do as you're told. Do you understand?

CINDERELLA: Yes, Stepmother.

STEPMOTHER: (*Handing her the broom*) You've spent enough time on those flowers. Here, take this broom and sweep the walk.

CINDERELLA: Yes, Ma'am.

STEPMOTHER: And you'd better do a good job, too.

CINDERELLA: I'll try my best.

STEPMOTHER: Make sure you do. (*She exits.*)

DIANNA: Goodness, but your stepmother is mean to you.

CINDERELLA: Sometimes.

DIANNA: I'm glad I don't have to live with her.

CINDERELLA: It's not always easy.

DIANNA: Well, I'll help. Maybe she'll still let you go to the fair.

CINDERELLA: Oh, no thank you, Dianna.

DIANNA: But I want to help you.

CINDERELLA: She'd just think I'm being lazy and trying to get out of doing my work.

DIANNA: She would?

CINDERELLA: Yes, she'd be furious with me.

DIANNA: All right, if you say so, but I wish I could do something. (*Offstage a handbell starts to ring.*)

CINDERELLA: Listen, there's a bell ringing. I think the vendor's coming. (*She starts sweeping.*)

VENDOR: (*Offstage*) Fresh fruit for sale. (*Entering*) Fresh fruit for sale.

DIANNA: What kinds do you have?

VENDOR: Apples, pears, peaches, plums.

DIANNA: I've been hungry for an apple pie. I'll take all of these. (*Pointing to the apples.*)

VENDOR: All right.

DIANNA: How much will it be?

VENDOR: That will be five lira. (*Handing her the apples.*)

DIANNA: Here you are.

VENDOR: Thank you.

CINDERELLA: I wish I could buy some fruit. It looks so good.

DIANNA: Doesn't your stepmother give you any money, Cinderella?

CINDERELLA: No, but she gives me food, and clothes, and a place to sleep.

DIANNA: Clothes! Why those are nothing but old rags!

(*Cinderella looks down, then shrugs her shoulders.*)

GEORGE: (*Hurrying in.*) I heard you calling. I want some of your pears. (*He points to certain fruit and the vendor takes them out.*)

STEPMOTHER: Cinderella, I caught you again. What do you mean by chatting with your friends when you have so much to do?

CINDERELLA: But I just finished sweeping the walk.

DIANNA: See how nice it looks?

GEORGE: It does look good.

DIANNA: She's been working all of the time.

STEPMOTHER: I don't want to hear another word out of any of you. Everybody leave right now.

DIANNA: Yes, Ma'am.

GEORGE: I'm going. I just came to buy some fruit. (*He starts to exit, then returns speaking excitedly.*) Hey, the king's messenger and his page are coming down the street.

STEPMOTHER: Probably wants us to pay more taxes.

DIANNA: What else could they want?

GEORGE: Do you think something has happened?

CINDERELLA: (*Hurrying in the direction from which the stepmother has entered.*) Isabella, Marybella. Come quickly. The king's messenger and page are on their way here. (*Isabella and Marybella come rushing out. A page with a bugle and a messenger with a large scroll enter.*)

MESSENGER: Hear ye, hear ye. On June 23rd the king and queen are having a ball in honor of Prince Raymond's 21st birthday. Everyone in the kingdom is invited to attend.

(*Speaking in unison.*)

ISABELLA: Oh, a ball!

MARYBELLA: How exciting!

GEORGE: This has never happened before!

DIANNA: I can't wait!

STEPMOTHER: Where will it be?

MESSENGER: In the king's garden, Saturday. Promptly at 8:00.

(They all start speaking excitedly.)

MARYBELLA: What shall I wear? Will my blue dress be all right?

ISABELLA: We must have new gowns. We want to look our best.

STEPMOTHER: Of course, darlings. Just imagine. My daughters are going to meet the prince!

CURTAIN

SCENE II. Cinderella's house the night of the ball.
   Cinderella is on the floor sewing up Isabella's hem.

MARYBELLA: *(Looking in a mirror.)* I just know the prince is going to fall in love with me.

ISABELLA: Oh?

MARYBELLA: Yes, I feel exceptionally beautiful tonight.

ISABELLA: You? Beautiful?

CINDERELLA: Of course she is.

ISABELLA: Why, I'm much prettier and I have a wonderful personality besides.

CINDERELLA: Your personality IS fine.

ISABELLA: I know!. . . . I'm just bound to be the one he'll like.

MARYBELLA: I wouldn't be so sure of myself if I were you.

ISABELLA: But there's no way he could keep from selecting me above all others.

STEPMOTHER: Well, I know it will be one of my darlings.

CINDERELLA: Please, may I go? I'll just sit at the back and watch.

STEPMOTHER: You?

CINDERELLA: Yes, I don't need to have a new dress. I can wear one of their old ones. Please. Everyone's invited.

STEPMOTHER: Don't be silly. Of course you can't go to the ball.

ISABELLA: (*Giggling*) Imagine Cinderella at the ball.

MARYBELLA: Who in the world would want to dance with her?

ISABELLA: Nobody, of course!

MARYBELLA: It's dumb of her to even want to go!

ISABELLA: Yes, ragged, ugly thing.

STEPMOTHER: Girls (*looking at her watch*), I just noticed the time. We must be going.

ISABELLA: Cinderella, fix my hair. (*Cinderella hurries to obey.*)

MARYBELLA: And tie my sash.

ISABELLA: Cinderella, bring my fan. (*Cinderella rushes offstage.*)

STEPMOTHER: And do hurry if you can.

MARYBELLA: Cinderella, bring my bag. (*Calling after her*)

STEPMOTHER: And fetch my shawl.

ISABELLA: Get some powder for my face.

STEPMOTHER: Cinderella, can't you hurry?

MARYBELLA: Why must you be so slow?

ISABELLA: The ball's starting at the palace.

MARYBELLA: It's time to go!

STEPMOTHER: (*As they are all exiting.*) I can't wait to see what the prince does when he sees you. (*Stopping and turning to Cinderella.*) Now I don't want you wasting any time while we're gone. Get busy and start cleaning the house. I want it spic and span when we get back. (*Cinderella nods. They exit.*)

CINDERELLA: (*Going to the door and waving to them.*) I hope you have a wonderful time. (*She turns, walks back into the room and starts to cry.*)

(*Her Godmother enters and tiptoes up to her.*)

GODMOTHER: Don't cry, Cinderella.

CINDERELLA: (*Turning in surprise.*) Who are you?

GODMOTHER: I don't think you'd believe me now if I told you. Why the tears?

CINDERELLA: Because I wanted to go to the ball. Everybody else is going and I have to stay here and work.

GODMOTHER: Don't cry any more, Cinderella. I'll help you.

CINDERELLA: You will?

GODMOTHER: Yes, you're going to get to go to the ball after all.

CINDERELLA: I am?

GODMOTHER: Yes.

CINDERELLA: How can I? I have nothing to wear, and the carriage has already gone, and I have to clean the house.

GODMOTHER: It's all going to be taken care of, but you need to help.

CINDERELLA: Of course.

GODMOTHER: I saw some mice in the trap. Go get them and bring them in.

CINDERELLA: Bring the mice in here?

GODMOTHER: If you please.

CINDERELLA: I don't understand.

GODMOTHER: Never mind, dear. Just do as I say.

(*Cinderella shakes her head, but exits then re-enters carrying the mouse cage containing six mice.*)

CINDERELLA: Here's the trap you wanted.

GODMOTHER: Good. Thank you. How many are there?

CINDERELLA: Six, but. . . .

GODMOTHER: Now don't worry.

CINDERELLA: All right.

GODMOTHER: Take the mice outside and put them on the road in front of the house.

CINDERELLA: (*Shaking her head.*) If you say so.

GODMOTHER: I do, and you must hurry or you'll miss lots of the ball.

(*Cinderella leaves then re-enters without the mousetrap.*)

GODMOTHER: Don't you have some pumpkins in the garden?

CINDERELLA: Yes.

GODMOTHER: Fine. Go out and get the very biggest one and put it right behind the mousetrap.

(*Cinderella leaves and re-enters.*)

CINDERELLA: I did just as you said.

GODMOTHER: Very good, dear. Now close your eyes until I tell you to open them.

CINDERELLA: All right.

(*Godmother waves her wand by the outside door.*)

GODMOTHER: You can open your eyes now. Come here and look out.
          (*Cinderella crosses to the door.*)

CINDERELLA: I can't believe it.

GODMOTHER: Yes.

CINDERELLA: The pumpkin and the mice are gone and there's a beautiful carriage with four white horses and two horsemen outside!

GODMOTHER: (*Nodding her head "yes." Then she looks critically at Cinderella's dress.*) Now I'll have to do something about those rags you're wearing. (*She waves her wand.*)

CINDERELLA: Why I can feel another dress underneath my clothes.

GODMOTHER: Let's see. (*She helps Cinderella slip off her ragged overclothes.*)

CINDERELLA: Oh, it's so pretty. I've never seen a dress as lovely.

GODMOTHER: (*Looking her over carefully.*) It's perfect. But, Cinderella, you're what makes it beautiful.

CINDERELLA: It's all so wonderful. I still can't believe it's happening.

GODMOTHER: You will. Now listen carefully. In the coach you'll find some glass slippers to go with the dress.

CINDERELLA: Glass slippers!

GODMOTHER: They should fit you just right.

CINDERELLA: Imagine.

GODMOTHER: Yes, go now, dear, and have a good time, but remember one thing.

CINDERELLA: What is that?

GODMOTHER: You must be gone by the last stroke of twelve or the coach will turn back into a pumpkin, the horses and coachmen into mice, and your clothes will become these ugly old rags.

CINDERELLA: Don't worry. I'll be gone.

GODMOTHER: Good. See that you are.

CINDERELLA: Now, won't you tell me who you are?

GODMOTHER: All right, Cinderella.

CINDERELLA: Good!

GODMOTHER: I'm your fairy godmother and I care about you very much.

CINDERELLA: You must. (*She goes to her and kisses her.*)

GODMOTHER: Run along now but be sure to be gone before the last stroke of twelve.

CINDERELLA: I promise. (*She starts to exit, then turns back.*) How can I ever thank you?

GODMOTHER: Just seeing you happy is enough. Goodbye, dear. Have a good time. (*Cinderella blows her a kiss and leaves.*)

CURTAIN

SCENE III. The palace.

PRINCE: I hope I meet that special girl tonight.

QUEEN: Then that's what I want, too.

KING: So do I, son.

PRINCESS: (*In a teasing tone*) And I really do!

PRINCE: Why?

PRINCESS: Because then if she'll have you, maybe you'll get married and move into a castle of your own.

PRINCE: (*Playfully*) Why you wouldn't be able to stand it without me.

PRINCESS: No?

PRINCE: You'd probably do nothing but sit and cry.

PRINCESS: Want to bet?

(*Princess makes a face at Raymond.*)

QUEEN: Now children.

PRINCESS: (*Turning around modeling her costume.*) Oh, mother, I love my new dress.

QUEEN: I'm glad you like it, dear.

PRINCESS: Do you like it, Raymond?

PRINCE: (*Looking her over*) Yes, even on you it looks nice.

PRINCESS: Oh, Raymond. What do you think, Daddy?

KING: You look beautiful in it.

QUEEN: I do hope that everything will be just perfect for Raymond's birthday ball.

KING: I'm sure it will be. All the staff has been working very hard.

COOK: (*Entering and bowing*) Everything is ready, Your Majesty.

KING: Very good, James.

PRINCESS: What are we having?

COOK: Turkey, roast beef, ham, cheese, fruit, and a huge birthday cake.

PRINCESS: How big?

COOK: As high as Prince Raymond is tall.

PRINCESS: Really? I bet it's yummy.

QUEEN: Is there plenty of everything?

COOK: Yes, Your Majesty, we've been preparing the food for days.

QUEEN: I hear the musicians setting up.

PRINCE: That means the guests will be starting to arrive soon.

PRINCESS: I can't believe the time's finally here.

QUEEN: Yes, and we must go and greet everyone.

KING: You're right, dear. (*They start to exit.*)

PRINCESS: Oh, I hope we all have a wonderful time.

PRINCE: You know what I hope!

CURTAIN

SCENE IV. The ball.

On stage are the Prime Minister, the page, the messenger, and extras as needed. Two large thrones are in the center of the room and there is a smaller chair on either side. Guests, as desired, are standing on either side of the thrones.

PRIME MINISTER: Presenting their royal majesties, King Harold and Queen Teresa of the house of Veryrich. (*The king and queen enter and are seated.*) Presenting the Prince of Friendship. (*Prince Raymond enters and goes to sit by the queen.*) Presenting the Princess of Laughter. (*The princess enters and goes to sit by the king.*)

(*As the following are introduced they slowly approach the throne, bow or curtsy to the royal family, then walk and stand on alternating sides of the thrones.*)

Introducing Lord and Lady Goodenough.

Introducing Master and Mistress Mayberry.

Introducing Master and Mistress Goldenhorn.

Introducing Master and Mistress Merryweather.

Introducing Mistress Pennypincher and her daughters, Isabella and Marybella. (*They enter nervously.*)

KING: (*Rising*) Ladies and gentlemen, welcome to the palace. We are pleased to have you here to honor Prince Raymond on his 21st birthday. The musicians will play now and we want you to dance, eat, and be merry.

(*Cinderella enters and curtsies before the royal family.*)

PRIME MINISTER; Introducing, ah . . . May I have you name, please?

CINDERELLA: (*Moving her hand to her head in confusion*) Ah . . .

PRINCE: (*Stepping forward*) It won't matter at all if you will please have this dance with me. (*She smiles at him, and he takes her by the hand and they start to waltz.*)

CURTAIN

SCENE V. The palace terrace.
   Cinderella and the Prince enter.

CINDERELLA: I'm having such a good time at your party.

PRINCE: I'm glad. So am I.

(*A clock starts to chime.*)

CINDERELLA: Is that eleven o'clock?

PRINCE: (*Looking at his watch*) No, it's twelve.

CINDERELLA: Oh! The time has gone by so fast! I hate to leave, but I must go.

PRINCE: But it's still early.

CINDERELLA: Not for me. I have to leave now.

PRINCE: Have to?

CINDERELLA: Yes, I love your party, the music, getting to meet your parents, dancing with you, but I'm already late.

PRINCE: But we're just getting acquainted.

CINDERELLA: I know, but. . . .

PRINCE: You just can't leave so soon.

CINDERELLA: I must. Thank you for a wonderful evening.

(*Cinderella runs off stage. The prince follows her, calling*)

PRINCE: Wait. Wait just a minute, anyway. I don't even know your name. Please come back. (*He comes back on stage carrying one of Cinderella's glass slippers.*) She lost her shoe and I don't know how to return it . . . I must see her again. She's the girl I've been dreaming about . . . Maybe I can find her with this. Yes, that should work . . . I know my father will help me . . . I have to get her back.

CURTAIN

SCENE VI. Cinderella's house.
   Cinderella is on the floor with a bucket and scrub brush. The others are seated.

STEPMOTHER: Cinderella, can't you work faster?

ISABELLA: She is the slowest person I've ever seen.

MARYBELLA: Isn't she, though?

ISABELLA: Terrible.

MARYBELLA: The ball was such fun, Cinderella.

ISABELLA: It's too bad YOU couldn't go.

STEPMOTHER: Yes, the food was marvelous.

ISABELLA: And the palace was gorgeous.

MARYBELLA: What a shame we didn't get to dance with the prince though.

STEPMOTHER: But, darling, he only danced with that one girl.

ISABELLA: I know.

MARYBELLA: Such a disappointment.

ISABELLA: I wonder who she was.

MARYBELLA: She looked like someone I'd seen before, but I can't think who it is.

ISABELLA: Well, she WAS beautiful.

MARYBELLA: Yes, and the prince certainly did like her.

(*There is a knock at the door.*)

STEPMOTHER: Cinderella, go answer the door. Somebody's waiting outside.

ISABELLA: For heaven's sake don't keep them waiting.

(*Cinderella hurries to the door then returns.*)

CINDERELLA: The king's carriage is outside. A page, messenger, and the Prime Minister are at the door.

STEPMOTHER: They are?

ISABELLA: Wonder what they want?

MARYBELLA: What could they be doing here?

STEPMOTHER: Well, tell them to come in, Cinderella.

ISABELLA: Don't keep them waiting any longer. (*Holding up her hands and rolling her eyes*)

STEPMOTHER: I simply don't know what I'm going to do with that girl!

(*They rise and start to straighten their clothes and hair. The Prime Minister, messenger, and page enter.*)

(*Stepmother goes to the Prime Minister and offers him her hand.*)

MESSENGER: I bring you tidings of the King. (*He starts to read from a scroll.*) Be it known this day that my son has found a shoe. To find the maiden who fits it is what he plans to do. When he finds said maiden, he wants her for his bride. To live happily ever after in his castle, side by side. Signed, the King.

PRIME MINISTER: I have come to see if any girl in the household can fit the shoe the page has. (*Motioning to Isabella*) You first, if you please.

ISABELLA: (*Giggling*) Oh, certainly, sir. (*She sits in a chair and the page takes the shoe for her to try on. The others watch anxiously.*)

PAGE: Fits like a cow in a baby's crib!

ISABELLA: Well, I never.

(*The others shake their heads "yes."*)

PRIME MINISTER: You next, young lady. (*He motions to Marybella to be seated. As before, the others watch anxiously.*)

MARYBELLA: (*Taking her seat*) Of course, sir.

(*The page tries the shoe. The others shake their heads "no." Marybella rises.*)

PAGE: Fits like an elephant in a carriage.

(*Roseanne comes hurrying in.*)

ROSEANNE: Will you try the shoe on me? I was out of my house when you came by there.

PRIME MINISTER: Certainly. We don't want to miss anyone.

(*She sits and the page tries the shoe.*)

PAGE: A tadpole in the ocean.

ROSEANNE: (*Rising*) Oh, and I was hoping it would fit.

STEPMOTHER: (*Coyly*) Well, if you want every lady, I'm sure you want me, too. (*She prances to the chair to be fitted.*)

(*The page and the messenger look at each other questioningly, then they look at the Prime Minister who shrugs his shoulders, and raises his hands to signal, "Why not?"*)

PAGE: It's just like a whale in a bathtub!

(*The others shake their heads "yes."*)

STEPMOTHER: Humph. (*Raising her head and shoulders haughtily, she stands.*)

CINDERELLA: (*Coming forward*) May I try the shoe on, please?

STEPMOTHER: (*To Cinderella*) Don't be ridiculous, nobody's interested in you. (*To the Prime Minister*) She didn't go to the ball. I'd never allow that. She's just a servant.

PRIME MINISTER: The king's orders are for every woman in the kingdom to try on the shoe.

STEPMOTHER: It's a waste of time for her to do it.

(*Cinderella goes to a chair and is seated. The page tries on the shoe.*)

PAGE: It fits!

MESSENGER: It fits? (*Leaning over to look more closely*)

(*The others lean forward, look, and shake their heads "yes."*)

PRIME MINISTER: (*Approaching Cinderella and studying her and the shoe.*) It DOES fit!

STEPMOTHER: It couldn't fit!

CINDERELLA: (*Taking the mate out of her pocket*) And I have the other one.

PRIME MINISTER: You do?

CINDERELLA: See, here it is.

(*The others start to talk at once.*)

MARYBELLA: She does have it.

STEPMOTHER: (*Fanning herself, as if to keep from fainting.*) I can't believe it.

ISABELLA: Of all people, CINDERELLA!

PRIME MINISTER: Messenger, summon Prince Raymond to come immediately. Tell him we've found the girl who fits the shoe.

(*Messenger exits then returns with Prince Raymond. The others curtsy or bow as he comes into the room. The Prince goes directly to Cinderella.*)

PRINCE: I'd know you anywhere.

CINDERELLA: Even in these rags?

PRINCE: Of course. They're not important to me. You are!

CINDERELLA: I'm so glad that you've come.

PRINCE: I had to.

CINDERELLA: How I've hoped that you would.

PRINCE: Now we'll go to the palace and make plans for our wedding. Do you think you'd like to do that?

CINDERELLA: You know I would.

PRINCE: (*Taking her hand to lead her off.*) Then come.

ISABELLA: I don't know why I couldn't be the one to marry him and go and live in a castle.

MARYBELLA: Or me.

PAGE: Well, you never know. Maybe if you'll be kinder to everyone you'll find a prince of your own someday.

CINDERELLA: Then you can live happily ever after, too. Just like we are going to do!

CURTAIN

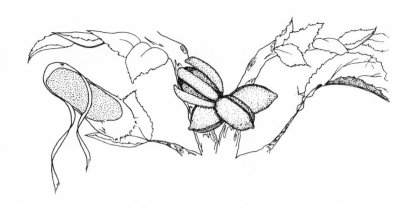

THE DANCING PRINCESSES

Cast of Characters

Willie, a page
Ansel, a page
The King
Prince, wanted the secret
Eric, a poor soldier
Alex, a dancing prince
Frederick, his brother
Adam, a dancing prince
Seth, another brother
Eugene, a dancing prince
Alfred, his brother
James, a dancing prince
Greg, his brother
Loren, a dancing prince

Nana, the princesses' nanny
Katya, a servant
Gretchen, a servant
Old woman, knew a secret
Elizabeth, Daddy's darling
Juliana, a snob
Dora, the silly princess
Patty, the pouty princess
Lorna, the organizer
Angela, the athlete
Katharine, older, bossy sister
Maria, very sweet and kind
Clarise, beauty-conscious
Bettina, a girl in love

Musician
Other musicians as needed

Production Notes

As written, the cast is for fourteen girls and fifteen-plus boys. It can easily be edited to become larger or smaller. More musicians, princesses, and princes can be added to increase the size. The original story had twelve princesses and this adaptation has ten. To make the cast smaller simply eliminate the characters in Scenes II and III. To do this, decide on the number of parts you need and give the extra person's lines to someone else. Additional information on adapting a script can be found in Step I of *10 STEPS TO A SUPER PRODUCTION,* "Modifying the Cast to Fit the Class or Group."

Any dance with fast music can be used in the dance scene. Music should be tape recorded on a machine that has numbers so that it can be properly cued. The music teacher is usually a great resource person for teaching the dance. Musicians should carry instruments and pantomime the playing unless you're extremely lucky and have a student who plays well enough to supply the music.

Discussion Questions

The following may be used for topics for creative writing or for discussion questions.

1. The princesses kept a secret from their father. When is it acceptable to keep secrets from your parents?
2. When is it a poor idea to keep a secret from your parents?
3. Who are some adults you can talk to about a problem if you do not want to go to your parents?
4. What can you do to make it easier to discuss an uncomfortable topic with another person?

5. How do you think the king was feeling during the play? Why? Go back and read just his lines. Did you like the king as a person? Why or why not?

6. What suggestions could you give the king to help him make his children more comfortable about coming to him with problems or secrets?

7. Do you think the king would have let the princesses meet the princes?

8. Write about your experience in keeping/not keeping a secret from your parents. How would circumstances have been better/worse if you had/had not told them?

9. Write a story about a boy/girl who keeps a secret from his or her parents.

10. Write a new ending for the play. Pretend that one of the princesses tells her father about her sister's secret activities. What happens?

11. In many societies it is traditional for parents to arrange marriages for their children. What is your opinion of this practice? What reasons can you give for having this practice? Write a story about a marriage arranged this way.

12. Pretend that either the king or Eric did not keep their word. Write a new ending for the play.

Enrichment Activities

Suggestions for the Teacher. An interesting time for the setting of *The Dancing Princesses* is France between the years 1775-1800. Have students do an activity from at least one category and teach the others in the class what they have learned. Children may work individually or in groups to complete assignments. Select one of the following projects to do:

1. Make a model of a carriage that could have been used in France during this period.

2. Make a relief map of France.

3. Make a model of Versailles.

   Write about one of the following topics. Have illustrations to show with your report.

1. French clothing between the years 1775-1800
2. Louis XVI furniture
3. Land in North America owned by France during this period (see the Louisiana Purchase). Include some of the travels and adventures of Sieur de La Salle in your report.

Write a report on one of the following:

1. France. Include information on the following: the people, climate, principal crops, exports, cities, and countries it borders.
2. Louis XV
3. Louis XVI
4. Marie Antoinette
5. The French Revolution
6. Bastille Day
7. Charles Dickens' *A Tale of Two Cities*
8. The Marquis de Lafayette
9. Benjamin Franklin

Do one of the following activities:

1. Write fifteen adjectives that describe the king. Divide them into groups: How you envision him physically; how you think he feels about what is happening; how he acts toward others.
2. Write five adjectives to describe each of the following people: Elizabeth, Patty, and Katharine.
3. Write a one-paragraph character description of Eric or the old woman.

The Dancing Princesses—Play Script

SCENE I. The king's quarters in the palace.
As the scene opens Katya, Gretchen, Ansel, and Willie are on stage. Nana hurries on. She is carrying a basket.

NANA: It's happened again!

WILLIE: You don't mean it!

NANA: (*Shaking her head sadly*) I do .

GRETCHEN: You mean the shoes?

KATYA: Of course she means the shoes, dummy.

GRETCHEN: Well, I wasn't sure.

WILLIE: The princesses wore them out again last night?

NANA: (*Nodding*) Yes.

ANSEL: But they just got new ones yesterday.

NANA: (*Sadly*) I know.

ANSEL: Are you sure?

NANA: Yes, see for yourself. (*They cross to the basket of shoes to examine them.*)

GRETCHEN: She's right.

KATYA: Look at these holes.

WILLIE: You'd think they'd been worn for months.

NANA: I know.

ANSEL: Are you sure these are the new shoes?

KATYA: Of course she's sure.

NANA: I thought maybe it was a trick, too.

GRETCHEN: And it's not?

NANA: (*Taking out a shoe*) No, I made a little red mark on each one only yesterday. See?

ANSEL: (*Looking at it*) Yes, it's right here by the heel.

KATYA: (*Pointing to the mark*) I can see it.

WILLIE: And I helped her mark them. Here's the little ''X'' I put on the toe of this one. (*Pointing*)

KATYA: Oh dear.

GRETCHEN: Then these have to be the new ones!

ANSEL: But how can that be?

NANA: (*Almost in tears*) I don't know.

WILLIE: You must not have locked the door.

ANSEL: Right.

NANA: But I did!

WILLIE: With the bolt on the outside?

NANA: Yes, and with the key, too. I kept it right here on my belt. (*She shows them a large key ring.*)

GRETCHEN: And you didn't let anyone have it?

NANA: No one.

KATYA: She even slept with it on.

NANA: (*Starting to cry*) Ohhhhhh, what am I going to do?

WILLIE: The king will be furious!

NANA: I know.

GRETCHEN: He may even say, "Off with your head!"

NANA: Nooooo!

KATYA: Gretchen, she doesn't need to hear that!

GRETCHEN: But, it's true.

WILLIE: You're right.

ANSEL: Yes, I heard him say only yesterday that if the mystery wasn't solved soon, some heads were going to roll.

NANA: (*Crying*) Oh, no!

KATYA: (*Going to her*) Poor dear.

GRETCHEN: But I still don't see how it could have happened.

WILLIE: I don't either. (*Shaking his head*)

ANSEL: Nor I. (*(Puzzled)*

GRETCHEN: It would take me months to get holes in my shoes like this.

KATYA: Aye.

NANA: How could they possibly wear them out in one night?

GRETCHEN: Maybe the prince who spent the night in their room to watch them will know.

NANA: I don't think so. He just shook his head when I went in to get the shoes.

WILLIE: (*Moving toward the door and looking out*) Watch out! The king's coming.

NANA: Ohhhhhh!

(*Nana hides the shoes in her basket. Ansel and Willie move quickly to stand at attention on either side of the king's chair. Katya and Gretchen hastily straighten out their clothes. They curtsy as the king enters.*)

KING: (*Looking at Nana*) Well, what is your news?

NANA: Your Highness, it is as always.

KING: As always? You mean the shoes are worn again?

GRETCHEN: Worn out is more like it, Your Majesty. (*Katya gives her a nudge.*)

NANA: Yes, Your Highness, and no one left the room.

KING: You're sure?

NANA: Yes. I locked and bolted it myself, and kept the key right here with me.

KATYA: That she did, Sir.

KING: I don't understand it.

GRETCHEN: Neither do we, Sir.

KING: What about the prince who was in their room guarding them last night?

NANA: We don't know, Sir.

KING: (*To Ansel*) Bring him to me immediately.

ANSEL: Very good, Sir. (*Bowing*) (*He exits.*)

(*The king moves toward his chair. Katya and Gretchen hurry to fluff the pillows and bring him a footrest. Ansel enters with the prince.*)

PRINCE: (*Bowing before the king*). I hear you wanted to see me, Your Majesty.

KING: Of course I wanted to see you!

PRINCE: I understand, Sir.

KING: Well, what happened? Did you see anything?

PRINCE: I tried, Your Highness.

KING: Tried? That is not enough.

PRINCE: I know, Sir. I watched and waited. . . .

KING: And . . .

PRINCE: And I saw nothing.

KING: Nothing!

PRINCE: Yes, Sir.

KING: Didn't you want the reward I had promised?

PRINCE: Oh, very much, sir. Any man would want to marry one of your beautiful daughters.

KING: But not enough to stay awake and see how they manage to wear out their shoes every night?

PRINCE: Oh, but Sir. I watched them. I really did.

KING: All night? Then how did this happen? (*To Nana*) Show him the shoes.

NANA: Yes, Your Majesty. (*She takes some shoes out of her basket and shows the soles of the shoes to the prince.*)

KING: These were brought here new yesterday.

PRINCE: But, Sir, how could that be?

KING: That's what you were supposed to have found out.

PRINCE: But I didn't even doze off until all the princesses were sleeping soundly. . . .

KING: Oh.

PRINCE: And then only for a few minutes.

KING: You failed. Just like the others!

PRINCE: But, Sir, how is it possible?

KING: I don't know.

PRINCE: Please. Just give me one more chance.

KING: No. (*To Ansel and Willie*) Take him out of my sight at once. (*Ansel and Willie move to his sides, facing the opposite direction and they start dragging him away.*)

PRINCE: But Your Highness . . .

KING: Leave at once, or I shall have your head.

PRINCE: Yes, Sir. (*As he is being pulled away he tries to bow.*) Thank you, Sir. I'm sorry, Sir.

KING: Fool!

GRETCHEN: (*Nodding her head*) Yes, Your Majesty.

KING: (*Rising*) My daughters are smarter than all of you.

KATYA: Yes, Your Highness.

KING: (*Leaving the room. The others curtsy or bow.*) I shall not stop until I have learned their secret. We'll see who can outwit whom.

(*Nana, Katya, and Gretchen follow the king out of the room.*)

GRETCHEN: I'm sure that you're much smarter than they are, sir. You'll solve the mystery. (*Katya kicks her to be quiet.*)

(The stage is empty for a few moments. Then an old cleaning lady with a mop and scrub bucket and some old rags enters the room and starts to clean. Several seconds pass and then Eric enters. He looks around and the old woman looks up in surprise.)

WOMAN: Oh, you startled me.

ERIC: I'm sorry.

WOMAN: What are you doing here?

ERIC: I'm waiting to see the princesses.

WOMAN: The princesses, huh?

ERIC: That's right.

WOMAN: I guess you're just like all the rest.

ERIC: The rest?

WOMAN: All the other princes who've come from all over to see if they can learn how the princesses manage to wear out their shoes every night.

ERIC: Well, you're right on part of it.

WOMAN: What do you mean?

ERIC: I DO want to solve the mystery and marry a princess. . . .

WOMAN: And?

ERIC: But I'm not a prince. I'm only a poor soldier.

WOMAN: You couldn't be. The king would never let you in.

ERIC: But he did. He said he was tired of princes. Not one of them could figure out what was happening.

WOMAN: And he decided to let you try?

ERIC: Yes.

WOMAN: Well, you won't have any luck either.

ERIC: Why not?

WOMAN: They're too smart for you.

ERIC: How do you know?

WOMAN: Because I'm the only one who knows what happens.

ERIC: Then why don't you tell?

WOMAN: Because nobody asked me. They think I'm only an old scrub woman.

ERIC: Well, I'm asking you. Will you tell me what happens?

WOMAN: Why should I?

ERIC: Why not? If I can marry a princess I'll become rich. Then I'll be able to help you.

WOMAN: But will you?

ERIC: Of course, I will.

WOMAN: How do I know I can trust you?

ERIC: Here. Take this. It's all I have that's of any value.

WOMAN: It's a gold ring.

ERIC: Yes, it was my father's. You can keep it until I get the reward money, then you can give it back to me when I pay you with gold.

WOMAN: That sounds fair.

ERIC: It is. When you get your money, you'll get your own house and servants.

WOMAN: That would be good. I wouldn't have to work so hard.

ERIC: Then you'll take the ring and tell me the secret?

WOMAN: I'm thinking about it.

ERIC: . . . And you will?

WOMAN: (*Pause*) All right. I will.

ERIC: Good. Now what should I do that the others haven't done?

WOMAN: You can not sleep a minute during the night.

ERIC: I didn't intend to.

WOMAN: And you must not let them trick you.

ERIC: How would they do that?

WOMAN: With a sleeping potion in the wine.

ERIC: So that's it!

WOMAN: Yes. Don't drink it, and watch carefully over everything they do.

ERIC: I will.

WOMAN: And bring back something with you, so that the king will believe you.

ERIC: Bring something back? I don't understand.

WOMAN: Yes. You must follow them.

ERIC: But they will see me.

WOMAN: Not with this. (*She digs into the pile of rags and brings out an old coat.*) Put this on when you start to leave and you will become invisible.

ERIC: Invisible?

WOMAN: Yes. No one will know you are with them.

ERIC: That's wonderful!

WOMAN: It is.

ERIC: And when I've learned their secret and get my reward, I shall repay you.

WOMAN: Make sure that you do.

CURTAIN

SCENE II. The princesses' quarters.
There is a mat and a table with a carafe. The princesses wear robes.

ELIZABETH: I wonder who dumb ole daddy has ready to guard us tonight.

JULIANA: Elizabeth, you shouldn't talk that way about Father.

BETTINA: But it's true.

KATHARINE: He's never been able to find anyone who has an idea about what we do.

DORA: That prince we've had the last few nights was kind of cute, though.

CLARISE: Yes. I sort of liked him.

PATTY: And he liked you, too.

LORNA: You could tell it by the way his eyes followed you wherever you went.

CLARISE: Yes, I noticed.

ANGELA: You bet you did!

KATHARINE: I was afraid you wouldn't let us give him the wine.

CLARISE: I really didn't want to.

DORA: But you did it.

CLARISE: I wasn't about to let him spoil our fun.

ELIZABETH: I'm glad of that.

LORNA: I don't think he even knew how long he was asleep.

ANGELA: (*Giggling*) No. He said something about just having dozed off!

DORA: I wish we could have seen his face when Nana showed him our shoes!

LORNA: I bet he turned white!

MARIA: You could tell he thought for sure he was going to get his reward. (*They laugh.*)

PATTY: I'll bet Daddy's mad about having to get us new shoes every day.

KATHARINE: You know it!

PATTY: He's probably going to start having us all wear workman's boots so that they will last longer.

DORA: Wouldn't that be terrible with our pretty dresses?

MARIA: Now, Dora, don't worry. I don't think that will happen.

LORNA: Hush. I think I can hear a key jangling down the hall.

KATHARINE: Must be Nana coming.

ANGELA: I DO wish they wouldn't keep us locked up in this room all the time.

JULIANA: It gets tiresome.

PATTY: It's like a jail.

ANGELA: But don't forget what happens at night. That's what makes it worthwhile.

LORNA: Sh! Angela, I hear the key in the lock.

NANA: (*Entering*) Girls, this is Eric.

ERIC: I'm honored to meet you.

CLARISE: And we're glad to meet you, too.

DORA: Are you a prince?

ANGELA: Dora!

ERIC: No, I'm just a poor soldier.

BETTINA: That's all right.

DORA: Yes, we might like you even better.

NANA: And you will be nice to him?

LORNA: Of course, Nana, we're always nice to our guards.

NANA: That's good to know.

ELIZABETH: Don't worry, Nana. We'll behave.

NANA: Fine. I'm glad to hear that. Well, goodnight, everyone, I'll see you in the morning.

MARIA: Goodnight, Nana.

BETTINA: Goodnight.

(*Nana leaves carrying the large key ring.*)

LORNA: Well, Eric, there's the mat where you are to sleep.

MARIA: I'm sorry it's not a bed like we have.

ERIC: I'm sure it will be fine. I have a knapsack for a pillow.

BETTINA: Have you heard terrible things about us?

ERIC: Not really.

KATHARINE: You didn't hear that we were selfish?

DORA: And mean?

CLARISE: And spoiled?

ERIC: Not exactly.

ELIZABETH: Good, because we're not. Are we, girls?

PATTY: No.

ANGELA: Of course not.

(*The others shake their heads, "no."*)

CLARISE: Just smart!

BETTINA: Sh!

LORNA: (*Going to a table where there is a carafe of wine, she pours a glass and takes it to Eric.*) Here. Just to show you how really nice we are. Have some of this.

MARIA: Yes. We don't blame you for your job.

LORNA: Here's a glass of our very best wine.

ERIC: How kind of you.

DORA: Try it.

MARIA: (*Watching him anxiously*) Do you like it?

ERIC: (*Holding the glass to his lips and pretending to drink*) It's delicious. I've never had any so good.

ANGELA: Good.

BETTINA: Then drink it all.

ERIC: Oh, I will. I just want to sip it, so I can enjoy it longer.

LORNA: I'll get you more when you want it.

ERIC: Fine. Thank you.

PATTY: (*Stretching, and pretending a yawn*) I'm getting sleepy.

MARIA: So am I.

JULIANA: Yes, it's about time for bed.

ANGELA: But first I want to take my exercises.

BETTINA: Me too.

(*Clarise, Bettina, and Maria start to exercise. While they are occupied the others watch and clap and count. Eric unobtrusively pours the wine into his canteen. He then lies down on his pallet.*)

LORNA: Want a little more wine, Eric?

ERIC: No, thanks. I'm already getting sleepy, and I'm supposed to stay awake all night and watch you.

ANGELA: Why that's not necessary.

ELIZABETH: Of course not.

LORNA: You just take a little nap while we exercise.

(*Eric closes his eyes and pretends to sleep while the others exercise. He starts to snore. The others giggle and tiptoe beside him to see if he is really sleeping.*)

DORA: The wine's all gone.

KATHARINE: Dead to the world!

ELIZABETH: Listen to him snore. (*Giggling*)

DORA: (*Picking up his wrist and letting it fall to the ground*) He won't wake up until early in the morning.

BETTINA: Did you see what pretty eyes he has?

MARIA: Oh, Bettina.

BETTINA: And he seems awfully nice.

LORNA: Forget it, Bettina.

KATHARINE: Let's get ready to go.

CLARISE: Yes. It's getting late. (*The princesses start to take off their robes. Underneath they are wearing party dresses. Elizabeth picks up a mirror from the table and looks at it.*)

ELIZABETH: I'm almost ready.

CLARISE: Does my hair look all right?

LORNA: Never looked better.

BETTINA: (*To Maria*) Will you tie my sash? (*Maria nods, crosses to her and ties the sash.*)

PATTY: My new shoes are a little tight.

MARIA: They'll loosen up soon.

JULIANA: Is everybody about ready?

CLARISE: You bet.

LORNA: I've been ready for hours.

JULIANA: All set, then . . .

PATTY: I am, if I can go barefoot!

JULIANA: No, Patty.

PATTY: All right. (She starts to put on her shoes.)

LORNA: Then I'll go open the trap door.

CLARISE: I'll help you. It's heavy.

(*They exit*)

BETTINA: (*Going over to look at Eric again*) He's sound asleep. (*She smiles at him sweetly.*)

KATHARINE: Then it's safe.

JULIANA: (*Calling from offstage*) Hurry, girls. We don't want to be late.

BETTINA: We're coming. (*All exit, except for Elizabeth.*)

ELIZABETH: Wait for me. I'm right behind you. Don't close the door.

(*She exits. There is the sound of a door closing. Eric sits up and looks around carefully. Seeing that there is no one left, he rises quickly.*)

ERIC: They're gone. Now I must put on the coat that makes me invisible, find the trap door in that closet, and follow them. (*He takes the coat out of his knapsack and puts it on. As he walks toward the door where the others have exited, he says:*) This should be a very interesting evening.

CURTAIN

SCENE III. The underground garden.
    Three trees, one gold, one silver, and one with leaves that shine with glitter are on stage. The Princesses enter laughing. Elizabeth enters last, with Eric not far behind her.

JULIANA: We got here early, after all.

CLARISE: Good. Now, I'll have time to fix my hair. (*She fluffs it.*)

KATHARINE: You look beautiful, Clarise.

(*Eric, who by this time is following closely behind Elizabeth, steps on her dress. She pulls it, saying:*)

ELIZABETH: Quit stepping on my dress. You'll make me tear it!

(*She pulls harder on it, but Eric keeps his foot on her dress and laughs silently.*)

LORNA: Silly girl. There's nobody behind you! See for yourself.

(*Elizabeth turns around, sees no one, then turns back to the others in a puzzled way.*)

(*The others giggle. Eric tiptoes up behind Bettina and kisses her cheek. She frantically brushes it with the back of her hand, as if to get rid of an insect. Eric moves aside and laughs. Next he pulls on her sash and unties it.*)

BETTINA: Juliana! Quit untieing my sash!

JULIANA: But, I didn't!

BETTINA: Don't say you didn't! Look at it!

(*Eric puts his hand over his mouth to cover his laugh.*)

KATHARINE: You must have caught it on something.

MARIA: Never mind. I'll tie it again.

CLARISE: Well, I'm going to sit down and wait for them. (*She sits.*)

KATHARINE: Good idea. I will, too. There'll be enough time to be on our feet.

BETTINA: You're right about that.

(*As Maria is tying Bettina's sash, Eric slips up behind her and starts to tickle her.*)

MARIA: Quit tickling me!

ANGELA: I didn't touch you.

MARIA: Somebody did!

DORA: I don't know what's the matter with everyone tonight.

KATHARINE: I know. We're all jumpy.

LORNA: It's probably because the man who rowed us over said the boat seemed so heavy he thought there must be somebody else in it.

PATTY: But that's dumb.

DORA: Of course. Nobody else was in the boat.

BETTINA: Something's strange, though.

KATHARINE: No. We're just being silly.

MARIA: Listen. The boys are coming.

(*The boys enter, followed by several musicians carrying instruments.*)

ALEX: Sorry we kept you waiting.

FREDERICK: Mother kept talking and talking all during dinner.

ADAM: And we didn't want to make her suspicious.

SETH: But we're finally here.

LOREN: And I'm ready to dance. (*He goes to Patty.*) Are you?

PATTY: (*Nodding*) Yes, even if my feet hurt.

EUGENE: Good. (*To Maria*) What about you?

MARIA: I could hardly wait for you to come.

ALFRED: Then, musicians, start the music.

ALEX: Yes. We're ready.

(*The boys each take a girl and form a circle. The music starts and they begin a fast dance. Eric stands at the side watching. After the music stops the dancers fan themselves.*)

ADAM: That was a fast one!

JULIANA: (*Laughing*) We're really going to wear out our shoes tonight!

PATTY: I'm tired and my shoes hurt my feet.

JAMES: Why don't we go get something to drink before the next one then?

CLARISE: Good idea.

KATHARINE: I'm ready.

EUGENE: Then come on.

GREG: So we can get back and dance some more.

SETH: But first the lemonade.

(*The dancers and musicians exit.*)

ERIC: So that's how they wear out their shoes! I can understand now. . . . The old woman said I should take back some souvenirs so that the king would believe me. Guess I'd better do it. (*He goes to the silver tree.*) Here's a silver leaf. I'll take that. (*He plucks a leaf and then goes to the golden tree and looks at it.*) This leaf's all gold. That's really amazing. (*He takes a gold leaf.*) Now for this last tree. Why these leaves are covered with diamonds. Just this leaf is worth a fortune. Wait until the king sees this! He'll believe whatever I tell him!

CURTAIN

SCENE IV. The king's quarters.

The scene is the same as Scene I. A throne, or king's chair, is the only furniture. Katya, Gretchen, Ansel, and Willie are talking. The old woman is on her hands and knees scrubbing the floor, a suds bucket next to her. Nana enters carrying the basket of shoes.

KATYA: What happened last night?

WILLIE: How did it go?

NANA: The same as always.

GRETCHEN: It was?

ANSEL: Their shoes were worn out AGAIN?

NANA: Again.

GRETCHEN: And everything was all locked up?

NANA: Yes, and I kept the key . . . but look. (*She holds up a shoe that she takes from her basket. The others move to look at it.*)

WILLIE: They're the new ones, too. Here's a little mark I made. (*The others crowd close to look.*)

NANA: What am I going to do?

KATYA: (*Crossing to her*) Oh, you poor thing. (*The king enters. The men stand at attention. The women curtsy.*)

KING: Well, what happened last night?

NANA: Oh, King. It was as always.

KING: Again.

NANA: Again. See here are the shoes I gave them only yesterday.

KING: I can't believe it.

NANA: Nor I, Your Majesty.

KING: They were locked in with the door bolted?

NANA: And I kept the key.

KING: This has to end! What did Eric, the soldier, say?

NANA: I haven't talked to him. He was asleep, just like the others when I went into the room.

KING: Asleep was he?

NANA: Yes.

KING: That's what always happens. No wonder I can't learn about what's going on.

NANA: Yes, Your Highness. (*Shaking her head*)

KING: Bring him to me at once. This one will not go unpunished.

(Willie and Ansel bow to the king and leave. The king crosses to his chair and sits. Eric enters with Willie and Ansel on either side.)

KING: You seem sleepy, soldier.

ERIC: Yes, I was up all last night.

KING: A soldier should be used to that.

ERIC: Oh, I am, Sir. I just dozed off.

KING: And I suppose you have no idea how my daughters managed to wear out their shoes again last night.

ERIC: But I do, Sir.

KING: You do?

ERIC: Yes, I do. They slip out through a trap door in their closet and go to a land far under the ground where they meet young men and dance until dawn.

KING: Unbelievable!

ERIC: Yes, Sir, but it's the truth!

KING: And what do you have as proof!

(At this the old woman looks up and stares attentively.)

ERIC: Sir, there are three very special trees where they meet.

KING: There are?

ERIC: Yes. One has silver leaves, another has gold leaves, and the third has leaves covered with diamonds.

KING and OTHERS (*in unison*): DIAMONDS?

ERIC: And I brought back a leaf from each tree.

KING: If you are telling the truth you may keep the leaves.

ERIC: It is the truth, Sir.

KING: Then let me see them.

ERIC: Here they are, your Highness

(*The king examines the leaves carefully. He tries to bite on the gold and silver ones. The others watch anxiously.*)

KING: They are real, and they are yours, as I promised. (*He hands them to Eric.*)

ERIC: Thank you, your Majesty.

KING: Do you want the rest of your reward?

ERIC: Of course I do, your Highness.

KING: Then you shall have one of my daughters for your wife. You may think about it, and then tell me whom you have selected.

ERIC: I don't need to think about it any more, Sir, my mind is already made up.

KING: It is?

ERIC: Yes.

KING: All right. (*To Nana*) Go get the girls and bring them to me at once.

NANA: Very good, Sir. (*She curtsies, then exits.*)

(*Eric crosses to the old woman and gives her the golden leaf. She smiles and gives him back his ring, which she has on a chain around her neck. As this is taking place the king is talking:*)

KING: (*Rising*) Thought they could outsmart their father, did they? Well, I'll show them. Who would have ever thought about them dancing all night in an underground room? One thing's certain. They won't be needing so many pairs of shoes anymore.

(*The princesses enter accompanied by Nana.*)

ELIZABETH: Daddy, you woke us up, and I was sound asleep.

KATHARINE: We all were.

KING: Tired out, I imagine, after dancing all night.

JULIANA: Dancing?

ANGELA: What do you mean?

(*Bettina smiles sweetly at Eric, who returns her smile.*)

KING: I think you know what I mean.

MARIA: Oh.

KING: Your secret has been found out.

DORA: It has?

KING: Yes. No longer shall you be able to slip away to the land that is underground.

ELIZABETH: But Father . . .

KING: The trap door will be nailed shut so you will not be able to open it. (*The others comment in unison:*)

PATTY: Oh, no, Daddy!

MARIA: Would you really do that?

CLARISE: Please don't, Daddy.

ELIZABETH: I can't believe you'd be so mean!

KING: Believe it. You'll go no more.

DORA: Daddy, that's terrible!

KING: You will all settle down and be good princesses and marry the man I choose for you.

JULIANA: But Father . . .

KING: And the first man is here now.

BETTINA: He is? Is it Eric?

KING: Yes, Eric. He is the one who learned your secret.

KATHARINE: He did?

KING: Yes, and I told him he could select whichever one of you pleases him most.

BETTINA: You did?

ERIC: (*Stepping forward*) Yes, he did, and you, Bettina, are the one I choose. Is that agreeable with you?

BETTINA: Oh, yes. I was hoping it would be me.

ERIC: Then I have your permission, your Majesty.

KING: Naturally. I always keep my word.

ERIC: (*Crossing to Bettina*) Then you will be my love, and my bride.

BETTINA: Yes, Eric. (*Happily.*)

KING: And this will forever end the nights of the dancing princesses!

CURTAIN

THE PIED PIPER OF HAMELIN

Cast of Characters

Sigfried, a city commissioner
Ludwig, a city commissioner
Johann, a city commissioner
Herman, a city commissioner
The Mayor, of Hamelin
Fritz, a city clerk
Peter, a handicapped boy
Andrew, an angry citizen
Klaus, Maria's friend
Carl, friend of Klaus
The Pied Piper

Frieda, a Hamelin resident
Marta, an angry woman
Louisa, one of the mob
Wilhelmina, an angry citizen
Elsbet, Hamelin resident
Irene, an irate woman
Katinka, one of the mob
Elsa, a Hamelin resident
Lorna, one of the mob
Gretchen, an angry woman
Gretel, Anna's friend
Anna, Maria's mother
Maria, a little girl
Sarah, Maria's friend

Production Notes

The Pied Piper of Hamelin was written for ten boys and fourteen girls. If a larger cast is needed, more roles can be added in all scenes. These may be walk-on roles with no speaking parts, or actors may be given some of the lines of the other characters. If more boys' roles are needed and fewer girls' parts, change the names and let the women become men. The cast may be reduced by writing out characters and giving their lines to others. This will work well on the first ten female parts.

Discussion Questions

The following questions may be used for discussion or as topics for creative writing.

1. At the beginning of the play Sigfried is running away from the angry mob. When is it a good idea to try to forget or run away from our problems? When should we face them or try to accept what is happening?
2. The mayor and the council did not tell the townspeople the truth about the Rat Bat. Why should people tell the truth?
3. When Peter wanted to help he was not allowed to. Should we let handicapped people do things for themselves or always help them in any way we can?
4. When Peter wanted to play with the other children they would not let him. How do you think this made him feel? Have you ever wanted to play with other children when they would not let you? How did this make you feel? What can you do if this happens?
5. Nobody would listen to Peter when he wanted to tell them about the Rat Bat. Why do you think this happened? Have you ever had a time when you could not get an adult to listen

to you? Is there anything that children can do to get adults to listen to them?

6. The council was actually stealing from the Pied Piper when they would not pay him the money they had promised him. Do you think this made it all right for the Pied Piper to steal the town's children?

7. The mayor and the council did not live up to their promises to the Pied Piper or the townspeople. Why is it important to do what we say we are going to do?

8. Would you like to go to the place the children were going? Why, or why not? Write a story about something that happens there.

9. Make an imaginary telecast from Hamelin. Have interviews with the Pied Piper, the mayor, council members, and townspeople.

Enrichment Activities

Suggestions for the teacher. The Pied Piper is set in Germany. Assign or have students select an activity from each category and explain or report to the class what they have learned. Students may do the assignment individually or as teams.

Do one of the following projects:

1. Dress a doll in traditional German clothing.
2. Make a model of the Bavarian Alps.
3. Make a map of Germany and show the following cities: Hamelin, Berlin, Hamburg, Frankfurt, and Munich.
4. Make a map of Germany showing the land regions.
5. Make a poster advertising the play *The Pied Piper*. Use your imagination about the time and place.
6. Make illustrations of the Mouser Louser and Rat Bat.
7. Make a peep box scene of the children going into the mountain or the land inside. Cut a window out of the end of a shoe box. Make a scene facing the window. Put light-

colored tissue paper or plastic over the top of the box. Look through the window to view your accomplishments.

Write a report on one of the following topics:

1. Germany. Include climate, principal exports, manufacturing, and agriculture.
2. German foods
3. German cars
4. Johannes Gutenberg
5. Ludwig van Beethoven
6. Johannes Brahms
7. Richard Wagner
8. Opera

Do one of the following activities:

1. Write a newspaper article telling about the events that took place in Hamelin.
2. Write another ending to the story.
3. Write a story about a handicapped boy or girl.
4. Write another version of *The Pied Piper*. Set the play in the United States in modern times.

The Pied Piper of Hamelin—Play Script

SCENE I. A room in the City Hall of Hamelin. There is a long table with five chairs behind it on stage left. On stage right there is a bench. The mayor and three of his city commissioners are sitting at the table when Herr Sigfried enters breathlessly.

SIGFRIED: (*Dashing to the table and starting to pull it toward the door.*) Hurry. Help me move this table in front of the door.

LUDWIG: But that thing is heavy.

SIGFRIED: That's why I need you. Hurry! (*Pulling harder*)

JOHANN: But, Sigfried, why move the table?

SIGFRIED: To save us!

MAYOR: Now calm yourself, Sigfried. You're all excited for nothing.

SIGFRIED: Nothing!

HERMAN: And you're white as chalk.

LUDWIG: Except for his nose, which seems a little redder than usual.

SIGFRIED: Nose! Oh, my nose!

HERMAN: What's the matter with your nose?

SIGFRIED: There will be plenty wrong if you don't help.

HERMAN: Help with your nose?

SIGFRIED: No, help me! (*Trying to pull the table. The others watch.*)

MAYOR: Now, my dear fellow. Of course we'll help, when you start making some sense.

LUDWIG: But at the moment you must surely realize . . .

SIGFRIED: REALIZE! I realize that it will soon be too late because you're just standing there refusing to do as I ask.

HERMAN: But Sigfried . . .

SIGFRIED: Well, when your ears are gone . . .

HERMAN: My ears?

SIGFRIED: And the mayor's fat stomach.

MAYOR: My, er, stomach?

SIGFRIED: And your fingers . . .

JOHANN: What ARE you talking about?

SIGFRIED: The mob that's coming.

HERMAN: What mob?

SIGFRIED: The one with the rolling pins and knives and clubs that says all of us will be in pieces before they've finished.

JOHANN: Oh, me. In pieces, huh? Maybe we should help him.

LUDWIG: Yes. Have they found out about the money?

HERMAN: And ask questions later. (*He starts to help move the table.*)

MAYOR: Perhaps you're right.

SIGFRIED: I know I'm right. They know we've been lying.

LUDWIG: Uh oh. And now they're coming to get us and since there's no key we can't keep them out.

(*There is a knock outside the door.*)

FRITZ: It's me, Fritz. I need to talk to you.

MAYOR: Yes, Fritz.

FRITZ: Your Honor, there's a big crowd coming across the square. They should be here any minute.

HERMAN: Do they look angry?

FRITZ: Pretty angry.

SIGFRIED: I told you.

LUDWIG: Why don't we climb out the window? (*Crossing the stage*)

MAYOR: Now wait a minute.

JOHANN: We don't have time to spare.

MAYOR: That's right. We'll just have to outthink them.

JOHANN: What do you mean?

MAYOR: I mean looking like we're guilty will just make it worse.

SIGFRIED: What do you want us to do then?

MAYOR: Just sit down in your places and help me talk to them.

SIGFRIED: I'd rather run away.

HERMAN: So would I.

MAYOR: Fritz. Go show them in and act like we're glad to see them.

FRITZ: I guess I can try. (*He exits.*)

MAYOR: (*Calling after him*) You'd better.

JOHANN: Let's get the table back in place. (*They go to push it back to its original location, then seat themselves on either side of the mayor.*)

FRIEDA: And we demand to see the mayor and his council immediately.

FRITZ: They'll be happy to see you. In fact, they've been waiting for you to get here. They're anxious to talk to you.

MARTA: I'll bet they are.

LOUISA: That's for sure.

FRITZ: Come right this way.

WILHELMINA: Try to stop us.

FRITZ: Oh, I wouldn't dream of trying.

(*The group of angry-looking men and women push their way into the room.*)

MAYOR: Good afternoon. How nice to see you.

ELSBET: You think so?

MAYOR: It's a pleasure to have you here.

IRENE: You won't think that for long!

MAYOR: What can we do for you?

MARTA: What can you do?

LOUISA: You can get rid of the rats.

MAYOR: I can assure you there's nothing that we want to do more.

FRIEDA: They just ate all the tarts and cakes in the window of our bakery.

WILHELMINA: And they're building nests in our best clothes.

MARTA: They're playing hide-and-seek in our attic. We can't sleep at night for all the noise they make.

ELSBET: The streets aren't even safe. A big one bit our cat!

LUDWIG: Bit your cat?

ELSBET: Yes, a delicate animal with long gray fur and a bushy tail.

HERMAN: And a rat bit her?

KATINKA: In two places. I saw them myself.

SIGFRIED: Aren't cats supposed to catch mice?

IRENE: NORMAL cats and NORMAL mice.

MARTA: But these are monstrous. And they hate us.

ELSBET: And you can't frighten them away.

ELSA: Just today I was hanging out clothes to dry and four rats followed right behind me and chewed the clothes off the pins as fast as I could get them hung up.

MAYOR: This is a very sad state of affairs.

MARTA: Indeed it is.

KATINKA: They've ruined our town.

ELSA: And our homes.

WILHELMINA: And our shops.

FRIEDA: And our lives!

LUDWIG: These are trying times.

WILHELMINA: Even our dogs are afraid.

FRIEDA: They refuse to go on walks.

IRENE: Who wouldn't? The rats are bigger than they are.

JOHANN: This is true?

IRENE: You know it is.

LOUISA: The poison you gave them made them bigger and stronger.

KATINKA: And meaner.

GRETCHEN: It's terrible.

MARTA: That it is.

IRENE: One even ran up the flagpole and chewed off the Hamelin flag this very morning.

WILHELMINA: It's a sad day when you think of our town and no flag.

HERMAN: That it is.

ELSA: We demand that you do something. (*Shaking a rolling pin*)

MAYOR: Nothing would please me more.

FRIEDA: Immediately. (*Ignoring him*)

MAYOR: Certainly, what do you suggest?

MARTA: That you get rid of the rats.

ELSBET: Or we'll get rid of you.

MAYOR: Now what would that accomplish?

HERMAN: Surely, you must know that we've been giving this matter all of our thoughts.

LUDWIG: Oh yes, indeed.

SIGFRIED: Night and day.

MAYOR: And having extra council sessions, too.

LOUISA: Probably just playing cards.

MAYOR: Playing cards!

LUDWIG: At a serious time like this?

LORNA: I wouldn't put it past you.

IRENE: Nor would I.

GRETCHEN: And we want something done.

ELSBET: Now.

FRIEDA: Yes, now.

KATINKA: If not sooner.

MAYOR: We can assure you that we're working on it.

LUDWIG: All the time.

SIGFRIED: Every minute.

HERMAN: The problem never leaves our minds.

MAYOR: And just today we got some exciting news.

LUDWIG: We did?

MAYOR: We did. All the way from Amsterdam.

LUDWIG: Oh, yes.

MAYOR: We learned about the Rat Bat that they have.

ELSBET: Rat Bat?

SIGFRIED: It just may solve our problem.

KATINKA: Wouldn't that be wonderful?

PETER: Watch out. It's probably a trick.

MAYOR: How COULD you think that?

WILHELMINA: It was easy.

MAYOR: They tell us the Rat Bat will get rid of the rats in a few days.

ELSA: But that's what you said about the Mouser Louser.

IRENE: And that was useless.

LOUISA: It just made more rats come.

ELSBET: And worse ones.

MAYOR: The mayor of Amsterdam himself has given his assurance.

GRETCHEN: But can we trust him?

LUDWIG: Most assuredly.

MAYOR: There is, however, one problem.

LORNA: And that is?

MAYOR: The Rat Bat will cost money.

LOUISA: How much?

SIGFRIED: More than the city council has.

LUDWIG: Oh, yes.

ANDREW: How much?

MAYOR: Five hundred marks.

ELSBET: That'a lot.

FRIEDA: A whole lot.

WILHELMINA: Still . . . The rats have ruined our businesses.

HERMAN: And with them gone, everything will be all right.

GRETCHEN: If they go.

KATINKA: Our worries will be over.

PETER: I don't think we should trust them.

MAYOR: I'm hurt.

SIGFRIED: We all are.

HERMAN: How could you doubt us?

ELSA: How can we trust you?

ELSBET: I don't think that we have any choice.

GRETCHEN: We have to do something.

LORNA: Yes. This can't go on.

FRIEDA: Remember what it was like when we didn't have to live with all these rats?

IRENE: Everything was nice and easy.

MARTA: And there weren't rats in everything we owned.

ELSA: I think we must give them the money.

LOUISA: And take a chance.

WILHELMINA: I say yes.

GRETCHEN: How long will it take to get the Rat Bat?

MAYOR: Less than a week.

ELSBET: And our troubles will be over.

FRIEDA: I say let's do it.

IRENE: Here's my part. (*She goes to the table and puts money on it.*)

MARTA: And mine. (*Putting down her money*)

LOUISA: I guess I'll go along with them. (*Going to the table*)

GRETCHEN: But if this doesn't work, it will be too bad for you and the council, Mr. Mayor.

MAYOR: You have nothing to worry about now.

ELSA: That's what you think.

GRETCHEN: Don't forget. (*Shaking her rolling pin at him*) We know how to use these.

LORNA: Yes, we do.

MARTA: And we will.

GRETCHEN: It might even be fun!

MAYOR: Don't worry.

HERMAN: Everything will be fine now.

WILHELMINA: It better be.

(*The others put money on the table and start to leave.*)

FRIEDA: We'll be waiting and watching.

MAYOR: Good. You do that.

LOUISA: We will.

HERMAN: Thank you for coming.

LUDWIG: We'll get right on it.

ELSBET: You'd better.

(*The mob exits. Peter, a handicapped boy, is still seated on the floor. He slowly pulls himself up. The Mayor and the City Council are looking at each other and do not see him.*)

MAYOR: (*Laughing*) We got rid of them!

SIGFRIED: But for how long?

MAYOR: Long enough.

LUDWIG: What is this Rat Bat?

MAYOR: It's nothing. I made it all up.

HERMAN: Oh, no.

JOHANN: You didn't.

MAYOR: I had to.

SIGFRIED: But what are we going to do?

LUDWIG: We'll take the money and leave Hamelin.

JOHANN: And never come back.

HERMAN: Now that's an idea.

SIGFRIED: And we'll go to where there are no more rats!

LUDWIG: And wives!

SIGFRIED: And children.

MAYOR: You see? Everything is going to work out just fine!

LUDWIG: It could be the beginning of a wonderful new life. (*Picking up the money*)

JOHANN: This has ended up being our lucky day.

CURTAIN

SCENE II. The park in front of the city hall. Anna and Gretel are seated on a park bench knitting. Maria is sitting on the ground playing with a doll. Peter comes up to them.

PETER: I heard them talking. It's a trick.

ANNA: Oh, Peter, don't interrupt. We're busy.

GRETEL: So do you think that we did right to give the Mayor and the Council the money?

ANNA: I have my doubts. What about you?

GRETEL: But we had no choice. The rats are getting worse and worse.

ANNA: I know. What if the Rat Bat doesn't work?

PETER: I'm trying to tell you. There is no Rat Bat.

GRETEL: Or makes them worse, like the Mouser Louser.

ANNA: Yes.

GRETEL: Then we're going to have to get rid of the Mayor and the City Council forever.

ANNA: I agree, but what about the rats?

GRETEL: They're terrible.

MARIA: Mother, watch out!

PETER: A rat is climbing up on the bench!

(*Gretel and Anna jump up on the bench. Anna drops her ball of yarn and it rolls away.*)

MARIA: Go way, you horrible thing.

(*Peter takes his crutch and swings at the invisible rat.*)

ANNA: Stay away.

GRETEL: Leave us alone.

PETER: It's gone now.

GRETEL: Thank goodness.

PETER: (*Starting after the yarn*) I'll get the yarn.

ANNA: No, Maria, you go get it. You're so much faster than Peter.

MARIA: All right.

GRETEL: I guess as long as I'm up, I'd better be going. I have to get dinner fixed.

ANNA: And me, too. If the rats left us anything to eat.

GRETEL: Aye. You never know.

MARIA: Mother, may I stay and play a little longer?

ANNA: Yes, but watch out for the rats.

MARIA: Oh, don't worry. I'll do that.

PETER: And I'll help her.

ANNA: Doubt if you'd be much help.

GRETEL: Oh, but here comes my Klaus now. He's fast and he'll take care of her.

ANNA: Good. Now come along soon.

(*Peter looks down sadly. Klaus and several other children enter.*)

KLAUS: Hello, Frau Meyer.

ANNA: Good afternoon, Klaus. You'll help Maria look out for rats, won't you?

KLAUS: For sure. Won't we, Carl?

CARL: Do it all the time.

GRETEL: And be home before dark.

KLAUS: Don't worry.

ANNA: Then we won't. (*She and Gretel exit.*)

SARAH: Let's play jump rope.

MARIA: Sure.

(*The children get in places for jump rope, two hold the ends of the rope, one goes to the center to jump.*)

PETER: I can hold the rope for you.

KLAUS: No. Better let Carl.

SARAH: You probably wouldn't know how fast to throw it since you can't jump.

(*Peter sits and looks sadly on as the other children jump rope. As they jump, they shout different rhymes.*)

ALL: Baa, baa, black sheep. Have you any wool? Yes, sir. Yes, sir. Three bags full. One for my master. And one for my dame. And one for the little boy who lives down the lane. (*Another child enters the rope area and the first child goes to turn the rope.*)

ALL: To market, to market. To buy a fat pig. Home again, home again. Jiggety jig.

MARIA: Do any of you know that fellow over there?

KLAUS: Which one?

MARIA: The one with the red and yellow coat?

SARAH: And that funny hat?

MARIA: Yes, that's the one.

CARL: I've never seen him before.

MARIA: Neither have I.

KLAUS: Wonder what he wants?

SARAH: Who knows? Maybe we can find out.

KLAUS: Yeah. He's coming this way.

PIED PIPER: You look like you're having fun.

MARIA: Yes, this is one game the rats usually let us play.

PIED PIPER: The rats? They bother you a lot?

SARAH: I'll say. They're everywhere.

KLAUS: All over our fields.

PETER: In our houses.

CARL: And our stores.

MARIA: We can't do anything without them.

SARAH: And they're getting bigger and meaner all the time.

CARL: They'll bite anything. And we're getting more of them every day.

PIED PIPER: Sounds like you have a real problem.

KLAUS: Do we ever!

MARIA: We're supposed to be getting a Rat Bat from Amsterdam in a few days.

CARL: Yes. They say it will get rid of them.

SARAH: I hope so.

PIED PIPER: That's strange. I've just come from Amsterdam, and I never heard a word about a Rat Bat while I was there.

PETER: See? I tried to tell you.

MARIA: You didn't see or hear anything about it?

PIED PIPER: No, I didn't.

CARL: Very peculiar.

KLAUS: I'll say it is.

PIED PIPER: Can you tell me how to get to the City Hall?

MARIA: It's right across the street.

PIED PIPER: Do you know if the mayor is there?

CARL: Oh, yes, he's there.

SARAH: And the City Council, too. I saw them all go in.

PIED PIPER: Good. I think I'll go over and have a little talk with them.

CURTAIN

SCENE III. The City Hall.
   The same room as Scene I. The Mayor and the City Council are sitting in their seats around the table.

SIGFRIED: I think the people are beginning to get suspicious.

LUDWIG: What makes you think that?

SIGFRIED: Just this afternoon I've had three people ask me when the Rat Bat is due to arrive.

HERMAN: I've had some people ask me, too.

LUDWIG: They're really going to be unhappy when they learn there is no Rat Bat.

HERMAN: And never has been one.

MAYOR: I suppose you're right.

SIGFRIED: Yes, you can't honestly blame them.

MAYOR: Then I guess we'd better start planning our escape for tonight.

SIGFRIED: If we don't want to get killed!

LUDWIG: I am going to miss some of my family, though.

HERMAN: Me, too.

MAYOR: Well, that can't be helped.

SIGFRIED: We'll be rid of the rats.

MAYOR: That will be a blessing.

FRITZ: (*Entering*) Your Honor?

MAYOR: Yes.

FRITZ: There's a gentleman here to see you.

MAYOR: We're too busy right now.

FRITZ: But he says it's important. Very important. It's about the rats.

MAYOR: All right. We'll see him, but only for a few minutes.

FRITZ: Very well. (*He exits and re-enters with the Pied Piper.*)

PIED PIPER: Good day, Gentlemen.

MAYOR: Good day. (*Fritz exits.*)

PIED PIPER: I understand you have quite a problem with rats here.

SIGFRIED: Do we ever!

PIED PIPER: And that you've ordered a Rat Bat from Amsterdam.

HERMAN: That's correct.

MAYOR: It certainly is.

PIED PIPER: That's strange.

MAYOR: Why?

PIED PIPER: I've just come from Amsterdam, and I didn't hear anything about a Rat Bat.

LUDWIG: You didn't?

PIED PIPER: No, I didn't.

SIGFRIED: Not a word?

PIED PIPER: Nothing.

MAYOR: How unusual.

PIED PIPER: Not really.

HERMAN: What do you mean?

PIED PIPER: That there is no Rat Bat.

MAYOR: Really?

PIED PIPER: Right. But I can get rid of your rats.

LUDWIG: How will you do it?

PIED PIPER: That's my secret, but I will do it for one hundred marks.

MAYOR: One hundred marks!

PIED PIPER: Yes.

MAYOR: That's a lot of money.

JOHANN: True.

MAYOR: What do you think?

SIGFRIED: Are you sure that it will work?

PIED PIPER: You have my word for it.

MAYOR: Well, Council, what do you say?

ALL: Aye.

MAYOR: You heard our vote. You may proceed.

PIED PIPER: Very well. I'll be back soon.

MAYOR: We look forward to your return. Don't we, Council?

HERMAN: Very much.

LUDWIG: That's right.

(*The Pied Piper bows to them and exits. The Mayor and the Council hurry to the window.*)

SIGFRIED: Look at him.

LUDWIG: He's starting to play his flute.

HERMAN: How strange.

MAYOR: Yes, and listen to that music.

LUDWIG: It's very different.

JOHANN: But look out there. Do you see what I see?

SIGFRIED: Rats are starting to follow him!

LUDWIG: There are dozens of them.

SIGFRIED: More like hundreds.

JOHANN: They're coming out of the houses.

MAYOR: And out of the fields.

HERMAN: It's amazing.

SIGFRIED: They're following along right behind him.

JOHANN: Some of them even look like they're dancing.

HERMAN: The entire street is full of them.

(*The Mayor, carrying some binoculars he's gotten off the table, or out of a drawer, tries to see out the window.*)

MAYOR: Let me through. I can see better with my spy glasses.

(*They let him closer to the window.*)

HERMAN: What's happening now?

MAYOR: He's gotten down to the river.

SIGFRIED: And . . .

MAYOR: The rats are all jumping in!

LUDWIG: They are?

HERMAN: Are they swimming?

MAYOR: They don't seem to be.

LUDWIG: Look at the other side.

HERMAN: Have any made it across?

MAYOR: I don't see a one.

LUDWIG: You mean we're finally rid of the rats?

MAYOR: It looks like it.

SIGFRIED: And I don't see any out on the streets.

HERMAN: They must have all drowned!

LUDWIG: Yes. Now he's turning around and walking back this way.

JOHANN: Already?

MAYOR: That was so fast I don't think he deserves a hundred marks, do you?

HERMAN: No, it hardly seems fair for such a little bit of time.

MAYOR: And if we only paid him ten marks and kept the rest that we got for the Rat Bat . . .

SIGFRIED: We'd have all that money for ourselves.

LUDWIG: And we won't have to leave now.

JOHANN: Masterful!

FRITZ: (*Entering*) Your Honor. That man with the strange red and yellow hat is here.

MAYOR: Show him in.

(*Fritz exits and re-enters with the Pied Piper, then exits.*)

MAYOR: Well, that certainly didn't take long.

PIED PIPER: No, and the rats are all gone.

MAYOR: That is most excellent news, my good man.

SIGFRIED: Indeed it is.

MAYOR: We are very appreciative.

PIED PIPER: I'm glad. Now the one hundred marks, please.

MAYOR: But surely you realize that your price is outrageous.

PIED PIPER: It's what we agreed upon.

MAYOR: But you spent so little time. I'm sure you know that the little job couldn't possibly by worth more than ten marks.

PIED PIPER: Ten marks? You promised one hundred.

JOHANN: You're getting overpaid at ten.

PIED PIPER: But we had a bargain.

MAYOR: That we've thought better about.

SIGFRIED: That's right.

MAYOR: Ten marks is our final offer.

PIED PIPER: You won't change your mind?

HERMAN: You heard our mayor.

PIED PIPER: Yes, I heard him break his word.

LUDWIG: Just a misunderstanding.

PIED PIPER: No . . . and you'll be sorry.

(*The Pied Piper puts his flute to his lips and starts to play it as he leaves the room. The Mayor and the City Council hurry to the window and look out.*)

HERMAN: See those children playing in the park across the street?

SIGFRIED: Yes.

HERMAN: Look. They're starting to follow the Piper.

MAYOR: Like the rats!

JOHANN: Yes.

LUDWIG: Oh, no!

SIGFRIED: And there are more coming down the street.

HERMAN: It looks like all the children in Hamelin.

SIGFRIED: There's my little Hansel. Hansel! Hansel! Come back. Don't go with that Piper fellow.

LUDWIG: He's not paying any attention.

SIGFRIED: And the others aren't neither.

JOHANN: Look. Their parents are running after them, but the children aren't stopping.

MAYOR: This is terrible.

SIGFRIED: Yes.

HERMAN: The only one they're listening to is the Piper.

MAYOR: (*Looking through his binoculars*) The children are on the bridge now.

LUDWIG: Some have even crossed to the other side.

SIGFRIED: And some of their parents are coming this way!

HERMAN: Probably for us.

MAYOR: Do you know that mountain on the other side of the river?

LUDWIG: Yes.

MAYOR: I just saw a big hole open up and the Piper went in. . . . Oh, no!

JOHANN: What?

MAYOR: The children are following him into the side of the mountain.

HERMAN: This is the worst thing that could have happened.

FRITZ: Your Honor.

MAYOR: Yes, Fritz.

FRITZ: There's a crowd of people crossing the street and coming this way.

JOHANN: Like before.

FRITZ: And they look even angrier.

SIGFRIED: They couldn't.

FRITZ: They do.

HERMAN: They're coming toward the window, too.

MAYOR: We're trapped. (*A group of people enter the room. Peter, whom they have carried in on a seat made out of their hands, is at the front of the group.*)

NICKOLAS: Our children have gone.

FRIEDA: They've followed the Piper into a hole in the mountain.

LORNA: The hole closed up again in front of our very eyes.

MARTA: Now we may never see them again.

PETER: I tried to warn you.

LORNA: We know.

GRETCHEN: We wouldn't listen.

ANDREW: And now it's too late.

LORNA: This is awful.

IRENE: My baby's gone!

WILHELMINA: Peter, why didn't you follow the Piper?

PETER: I couldn't keep up with the others.

LOUISA: Why did everyone want to go?

PETER: I heard a nice voice calling me. It was telling about a wonderful place where everyone is always kind, and no one is ever sick, or tired, or poor. There are birds, and flowers, and fruits, and nuts, too. I wish I could have gone with the others.

ELSBET: We're glad you didn't. Then we wouldn't have any children.

KATINKA: We want you here with us.

NICKOLAS: You're the only child we have left now.

ANNA: And, Peter, I'm sorry I didn't treat you better before.

GRETEL: I am, too.

WILHELMINA: I guess we all are, but we'll make it up to you.

LOUISA: Maybe if we start treating everybody better, our children will come back.

LORNA: We could make this like the place you heard about in the song.

ANDREW: But first let's get rid of the Mayor and the City Council.

MARTA: Right.

MAYOR: But why us?

NICKOLAS: Because the Piper told us as he went down the steps that you'd cheated him out of his money.

SIGFRIED: Us?

ANNA: Yes, you.

GRETEL: You made him take our children, and we'll never forgive you.

LUDWIG: We didn't know that would happen.

ANDREW: But what you did was wrong and you knew it. Now, start leaving right this minute and don't come back.

MAYOR: Don't come back?

WILHELMINA: Right, or you'll get a taste of my rolling pin.

LORNA: And my butcher knife. Now leave. (*Some of the crowd start toward them.*)

MAYOR: We're going. Fast. Right away. (*He and the Council exit.*)

LORNA: And good riddance.

KATINKA: Here's to the new Hamelin. The town with the heart!

GRETCHEN: The town where people care about each other, and are kind.

OTHERS: Here's to the New Hamelin, and to Peter, our friend.

CURTAIN

SLEEPING BEAUTY

Cast of Characters

Edwin, a custodian
Jack, a custodian
Eugene, a custodian
Herbert, the cook's helper
Cook, the king's chef
King, Beauty's father
Horace, Madelyn's husband
Andrew, Pamela's husband
Page, the king's helper
Jason, a Servant
Arnold, the Prince's valet
Prince, in love with Beauty
Guard, as needed
Guard, as needed

Nanny, Beauty's nurse
Queen, Beauty's mother
Madelyn, family friend
Pamela, family friend
Alice, a good fairy
Angela, a good fairy
Anna, a good fairy
Alison, a good fairy
Amanda, a good fairy
Hortense, an angry fairy
Old woman, spins thread

Production Notes

A play for twelve boys and eleven girls. Other guards may be added in non-speaking roles in Scene I, if needed. The old woman may be played by Hortense in Scene III, and the part of Amanda may be eliminated in Scene II if fewer girls are required.

The dance of the fairies in Scene I should be done to slow, dreamy music. Ideally, their costumes would be made the same but of different colors.

Scene IV can be played most effectively if Arnold can carry a lantern to light the darkened stage.

Discussion Questions

The following may be used for discussion, or as topics for creative writing.

1. All the fairies except for Hortense seemed to belong to a group. How do you think Hortense felt about this? How do you feel about belonging to a group?
2. Did the fairies have a responsibility to make the king and queen aware of Hortense's feelings about not having been invited to the party?
3. Are group members responsible for the actions of others who belong to the group?
4. Have you ever failed to get an invitation you wanted to receive? How did you feel?
5. If you could give a child you love one gift of the type the fairies gave Beauty, what gift would you give? Why?
6. Which of the fairies' gifts do you think was the best gift? Why?
7. The first gift the baby received was to have beauty. Do you feel that this is important? Why, or why not?
8. Hortense seemed to believe that the others were making fun

of her. How does it feel to have this happen? Write a story about a child who is ridiculed.

9. How does it feel to be an outsider? Write a story about someone who wants to belong to a group but is not included.
10. Imagine that Beauty awakens from her one-hundred-year sleep and she is all alone. Write a new ending to the play.

Enrichment Activities

Suggestions for the teacher. For research purposes set the play in Spain between the years 1490 and 1610. Have students do an activity from at least one category and teach the class what they have learned. Assignments may be completed by students working individually or in groups.

Select one of the following projects to do:

1. Make a model of a ship a Spanish explorer might have used between the years 1490–1610
2. Make a relief map of Spain.
3. Make a model of an Alcazar castle where Queen Isabella's coronation occurred in 1474.

Choose one of the following to complete:

1. Make several illustrations showing the type of clothing that was worn in Spain between the years 1490–1610.
2. Design sets that could be used for Scenes I, II, and III. Color your illustrations.

Make one of the following:

1. A map of Europe in 1500
2. A map showing the voyages of Columbus, Magellan, and Vasco da Gama

3. A map showing the journeys of De Soto, Coronado, Ponce de León, and Cortés

Write a report on one of the following:

1. Christopher Columbus
2. Queen Isabella and King Ferdinand
3. Amerigo Vespucci
4. Vasco da Gama
5. Ponce de León
6. Ferdinand Magellan
8. Vasco Núñez de Balboa
9. Hernando Cortés
10. Hernando de Soto
11. Francisco Vásquez de Coronado
12. The climate, principal crops, manufactured items, and recreation of Spain
13. The contributions and changes made by the Spanish in the New World

Write ten adjectives that could be used to describe:

1. Hortense
2. The cook
3. The prince

Sleeping Beauty—Play Script

SCENE I. A large room in a palace. There is a baby's bassinet with a rocker near it on stage left. There are two thrones right. (Three men with mops and brooms are cleaning the floor.)

EDWIN: There shouldn't be any complaints about the floor this time.

JACK: No, the king said he wanted to be able to see his face reflected in it and he can now.

EUGENE: Can't really blame him for wanting everything to be perfect.

EDWIN: That's right. It's a special day for him and the queen.

JACK: I hear they're using gold plates and gold goblets!

EDWIN: The very best of everything.

EUGENE: Having things just right for the party means a lot to the king and queen.

JACK: Yes, they'd wanted their baby girl for so long.

EUGENE: And she's here and a real beauty, too.

EDWIN: I can understand why they're so proud.

JACK: She's something to celebrate, all right!

EUGENE: No wonder they call her Beauty.

EDWIN: Guess that about does it in this room.

JACK: Yes, and we better go over that hall again.

EUGENE: There's not much time before the guests start to arrive, either.
> (*The three men exit carrying their mops and brooms. Nanny, carrying a baby, enters from another door. Herbert follows closely behind her making faces and trying to get Beauty's attention. Nanny crosses to the bassinet on the other side of the room.*)

NANNY: Just a minute, Beauty, and you'll be in your nice bed.

HERBERT: (*Shaking his finger at her and smiling*) Or I can hold her.

NANNY: And wrinkle her new dress? I guess not.

HERBERT: (*To Beauty*) But you'd like it better with me holding you, wouldn't you, sweetheart?

NANNY: No, Herbert, she wants her own bed. (*Putting her in her bassinet*)

HERBERT: Says who?

NANNY: The one who knows her best!

HERBERT: Pooh! See this, Beauty? (*He dangles some keys over her bassinet.*)

NANNY: Herbert! Quit that. You'll bother her. (*Seating herself*)

HERBERT: No I won't. She loves it! See. Herbert knows!

NANNY: Stop it.

HERBERT: (*Putting his hands up on either side of his head like ears and moving his fingers as he leans over the bassinet*) See the horsey? Does Beauty like the horsey?

NANNY: (*Rising*) Herbert, now you leave her alone. (*She crosses to the bassinet.*) Precious. Is that silly old man bothering you?

HERBERT: Bothering! She's laughing! Look at her!

NANNY: She is!

HERBERT: Wanna see big old horsey dance? (*He turns around dancing.*) Horsey dance for little Beauty.

NANNY: You might frighten her.

HERBERT: She's too smart for that. Aren't you, Beauty?

NANNY: Darling, I won't let anything happen to you.

HERBERT: And I wouldn't either.

NANNY: Look at her smile.

HERBERT: That's because she loves me.

NANNY: Probably a gas pain!

(*Cook enters shaking a rolling pin.*)

COOK: I've found you!

HERBERT: Yes.

COOK: What do you mean slipping away and coming in here to play with Beauty when we have so much to do?

HERBERT: I wasn't gone long.

COOK: Long enough for me to do all of your work.

HERBERT: Now that's not true.

COOK: True enough. Now you get back to the kitchen or we'll have you for lunch!

HERBERT: Me?

COOK: You.

HERBERT: Just for taking a little rest?

COOK: Yes, when there's so much to do down in the kitchen . . . All those people coming for the christening and banquet.

NANNY: Come look at her in her new dress.

COOK: (*Crossing to the bassinet to look at the baby*) Oh, you are a little doll, aren't you?

HERBERT: And she loves me! I'm her favorite! (*He tiptoes around, shakes his finger to get the baby's attention.*)

COOK: Just because you spend all your time playing with her instead of working.

HERBERT: Not all!

COOK: Enough! Back to the kitchen with you right now.

HERBERT: I'm leaving. (*Starting to run out*)

COOK: You better be. (*Going after Herbert waving the rolling pin*) And fast, too, or I'll fix you. (*They exit.*)

NANNY: (*To the baby*) Now, darling, maybe you can get a little nap before the party starts. (*She goes back to her chair and sits down and starts to sing softly to the baby. The king and queen enter and Nanny rises and curtsies.*)

QUEEN: And how's my baby. Has she been good?

NANNY: Couldn't have been better, Your Majesty.

QUEEN: No crying?

NANNY: Our Beauty? She almost never cries.

QUEEN: (*Crossing to the bassinet*) My little angel.

KING: (*Following the queen*) Our Beauty.

QUEEN: Look, Albert, she's smiling at us.

KING: She is!

QUEEN: And she's so beautiful!

KING: Like her mother.

QUEEN: Thank you, Albert.

NANNY: Her new dress is lovely on her, too, Ma'am.

QUEEN: Isn't it though? It took the seamstress weeks to make it.

NANNY: And it shows, too, Your Majesty. I'm sure it's bound to be the finest gown a little princess ever had.

QUEEN: I hope so. I want it to be.

KING: Nothing's too good for our little Beauty.

QUEEN: I do hope she'll behave at the party.

NANNY: Well, if she doesn't it will be a big change.

QUEEN: Yes, but the people might frighten her.

NANNY: Now don't you worry. I'll take care of her.

KING: I think she knows what we're saying. Look at her. She's laughing.

QUEEN: She is!

KING: Isn't she wonderful?

(*The page enters, crosses to the royal family, and bows.*)

PAGE: Sir, the guests are starting to arrive. Should they be allowed to enter?

KING: By all means. Come, dear, let's be seated.

QUEEN: Of course, Albert. (*They go to their chairs.*)

(*Madelyn and Horace enter. They are carrying a large package. The page follows them. Madelyn and Horace curtsy and bow to the king and queen. They give the page the package.*)

KING: At ease.

MADELYN: We've brought a small gift of welcome for the princess, Your Majesties.

QUEEN: That's very kind of you.

HORACE: Just a token of our esteem.

KING: Thank you. (*The king nods to the page who exits.*)

MADELYN: May we see the little love?

QUEEN: Of course, she's there in her cradle. (*They cross to the baby.*)

MADELYN: Oh, she's beautiful.

HORACE: Yes, a fine daughter you have there.

NANNY: And so good, too.

(*The page enters, followed by Pamela and Andrew. They approach the thrones and curtsy and bow. The king and queen smile and nod to them. They give the page their gifts. He exits.*)

ANDREW: A pleasure to be here, Sir.

PAMELA: Yes, we're excited about getting to see the new princess.

KING: She's our pride, you know. Really a wonderful baby.

QUEEN: Albert, you shouldn't brag so.

KING: But, dear, it's the truth.

PAMELA: Oh, I'm sure it is, Your Highness.

ANDREW: And I have no doubt but what you're right, Sir.

PAGE: (*Entering and bowing*) The fairies have arrived, Your Majesties.

QUEEN: Oh, Albert, they're here!

MADELYN: To give out their gifts and blessings.

PAMELA: I can't wait to see what they'll be.

KING: Show them in at once.

PAGE: Yes, Your Highness.

(*Background music starts to play softly. Four fairies enter and begin to go one by one to curtsy in front of the king and queen. A fifth fairy starts to enter, then goes back to the door calling:*)

ALICE: Angela . . . Angela. What's the matter? Why aren't you coming?

ANGELA: (*Entering but standing by the door*) It's because of Hortense!

ALICE: Hortense! She wasn't invited.

ANGELA: I know, but she's here. I just saw her!

ALICE: Are you sure?

ANGELA: I am, and she looked furious!

ALICE: She did! Oh, then she might harm the baby!

ANGELA: I know. That's why I'm going to stay behind to see what she's going to do.

ALICE: All right. That sounds like a good idea.

ANGELA: Go on, and don't tell anyone I'm here.

ALICE: Don't worry. I won't. (*Alice goes to the king and queen and curtsies low, then she joins the four other fairies as they start to dance around the room. When the dance is over the fairies are standing behind the baby's cradle. Anna steps forward waving her wand.*)

ANNA: My Princess, my gift for you is beauty. Although you are pretty now as a baby, your looks are nothing to compare with what they will be as you grow older. Throughout the land you will be known as the most beautiful person who has ever lived in the kingdom. Your lovely face will brighten every room you enter and make the dreariest days full of sunlight.

QUEEN: What a wonderful gift! Thank you.

KING: We appreciate the gift that you've given her.

PAMELA: Beauty is going to be a good name for her.

QUEEN: Just think, Albert, our little girl is going to be the most beautiful in all the land.

AMANDA: (*Stepping toward the cradle and waving her wand over it*) And my gift to you, my Princess, is the gift of laughter. Your presence will bring joy to the hearts of all who are near you. Your life will be filled with merriment, and you will receive as much happiness as you will give to others.

QUEEN: What a wonderful gift! Thank you, good fairy.

KING: Yes, you have our gratitude.

QUEEN: Albert, it's going to be such fun to watch her grow up! We'll have a very happy home because the good fairy says everyone around Beauty will be content and merry, too.

KING: What a kind gift you have given her. We will feel such joy watching her bring pleasure to others.

ALICE: (*Stepping forward and waving her wand over the baby's cradle*) And to you, my Princess, I give the gift of charm, which will so enchant others that it will be like a magic spell causing them to delight in just having you near.

QUEEN: Thank you very much, good fairy.

KING: We appreciate your kindness. My greatest wish has been to have our daughter admired and respected.

ALISON: (*Stepping to the cradle and waving her wand over it*) And my gift to you, little one, will be the gift of love. You will always be surrounded by those who love you greatly. Their love will fill you with happiness. Others will want to be near you to help you have the things you most desire.

KING: There is no gift you could give her that is greater than love.

HORTENSE: (*Entering and laughing wildly*) Ha! Ha! Yes, you've given her gifts, but they will not be with her long! I'll see to that.

KING: Not long? What do you mean?

HORTENSE: I mean, dear King, that your precious little daughter will only be with us a few short years and then she will die!

OTHERS: (*In horror*) Die?

HORTENSE: (*Laughing again.*) Yes, die!

QUEEN: But why are you doing this to her? To us?

HORTENSE: (*Sneering*) Because, Your Royal Highness, you did not see fit to invite me to your child's christening and the banquet.

QUEEN: But I didn't think you would want to come. You never go anywhere.

HORTENSE: I'm here, aren't I?

QUEEN: But you didn't send greetings when she was born like the others. I didn't think you cared.

HORTENSE: You lie. You didn't think I was good enough to come.

QUEEN: But that's not true.

HORTENSE: Well, you will live to regret your decision. She will die because of it.

QUEEN: Oh, no.

HORTENSE: Yes. Oh her sixteenth birthday she will prick her finger on a spindle and that will be the end of her!

KING: Oh, please. No!

HORTENSE: Oh, please, yes! That will teach you to treat Hortense as one not worthy of an invitation to your precious party! (*She exits laughing wildly.*) You will never forget me again!

QUEEN: (*Crying*) This is terrible.

KING: I can't believe what's happened.

QUEEN: Albert, surely you can do something.

KING: (*There is a pause and the king shakes his head.*) Page.

PAGE: Yes, Your Majesty.

KING: Go at once. Put the word out that every spinning wheel and every spindle in the country is to be destroyed.

PAGE: I'll leave at once, Your Highness.

QUEEN: But will that keep her safe, Albert?

KING: Of course it will, my dear.

ANGELA: (*Entering*) But not safe enough.

QUEEN: Oh, then won't you help us? Please. I beg you.

ANGELA: I will do what I can.

QUEEN: Please. Please do.

ANGELA: I can't take away Hortense's spell but I can change it.

KING: And you will?

ANGELA: I'll do what I can. The little Princess will not die. Instead she will fall into a one hundred years' sleep from which she can not be roused until a prince comes and wakens her.

CURTAIN

SCENE II. The palace sixteen years later.
    The room is the same as for Scene I, except the baby bassinet has been replaced by a table. Nanny's rocking chair is gone. Cook enters carrying a tablecloth. He goes to the table and starts putting the cloth on the table. His temples have been grayed so that he looks older than in Act I.

COOK: Herbert! Herbert! Now where is he? Every time I need him he's always somewhere else doing something he shouldn't be doing. (*He walks to the door through which he has just entered and calls.*)

COOK: Herbert! You get in here right this minute. Do you hear me?

HERBERT: (*From off stage*) Yes, I hear you. I'm coming.

COOK: And don't be poking along, either!

HERBERT: Me poke along, sir?

COOK: (*Walking back to the table but talking over his shoulder to Herbert*) Who else would I mean? Bring the candle holders and the centerpiece when you come.

HERBERT: Yes, Your Majesty.

COOK: And stop calling me ''Your Majesty.'' What if the king should hear you?

HERBERT: (*Entering with the candle holders and the centerpiece*) He'd probably just think that you were being unreasonable in the way that you were bossing me around, sir. (*Sarcastically*)

COOK: I have every right to order you around, and you know it.

HERBERT: I know you do, sir.

COOK: (*Smoothing the tablecloth*) Now put the centerpiece in the middle of the table and the candles on either side.

HERBERT: (*Places the centerpiece as instructed and puts the candles as close to it as possible*) This all right?

COOK: Oh, of course it's not all right! (*He moves the candles further apart.*) Like this. Don't you ever remember anything?

HERBERT: Everything you've ever told me.

COOK: That's a lie. How do I ever manage to put up with you?

HERBERT: Because you have to. Nobody else will put up with you.

COOK: Why ...

(*Beauty enters and they nod their heads to her.*)

BEAUTY: The table looks lovely, and everything smells so good in the kitchen. I'll bet you've been baking my birthday cake.

COOK: That I have, and it's a masterpiece, Beauty. This tall. (*Holds hands up to show a cake almost shoulder-high*)

HERBERT: And it has sixteen candles on it.

COOK: One for every year.

BEAUTY: You're always nice and do so many special things for me.

COOK: Nothing's too good for our Princess, is it, Herbert?

HERBERT: Of course not.

BEAUTY: But you spoil me.

COOK: We only give you what you deserve, Beauty. This is your special day.

BEAUTY: I know. I've been busy getting dressed for the party, or I would have slipped down to the kitchen to watch you decorate it, like I always do.

HERBERT: You look lovely, Beauty.

BEAUTY: Thank you, Herbert. (*She twirls around to show off her dress.*)

COOK: Well, I've finally found one thing he's right about!

BEAUTY: You know better than that!

COOK: All right, Your Highness.

BEAUTY: Now you don't have to call me that. Just because I'm sixteen doesn't mean I've forgotten how you used to let me stir the batter . . .

HERBERT: And lick the spoon, too!

COOK: But don't tell your mother.

BEAUTY: Don't worry. I'd never do that.

QUEEN: (*Entering. Her hair is now gray.*) Oh, there you are, dear. I've been looking all over for you. (*Herbert and Cook bow.*)

BEAUTY: Poor thing. I should have told you where I was going.

QUEEN: It's all right, dear. Let me look at you. You look wonderful.

BEAUTY: Thank you, mother. It's the beautiful dress you had made for me.

QUEEN: Such modesty! I'm glad you're ready because it's almost time.

COOK: Then we'd better be leaving, Your Majesty. (*Exits, pulling Herbert behind him*)

BEAUTY: I've really been looking forward to today and the party you're giving me. You've gone to so much trouble, though.

QUEEN: Nonsense. You only have a sixteenth birthday once, dear.

(*Two guards enter and stand at attention on either side of the door. They are followed by the King, Pamela, Madelyn, Horace, and Andrew. Their hair has also been grayed. Beauty crosses to greet them.*)

MADELYN: Happy birthday, Beauty.

BEAUTY: Thank you, Lady Madelyn. (*She goes to her and kisses her on the cheek.*)

PAMELA: Yes, a very happy birthday to you.

BEAUTY: And thank you, Lady Pamela. (*Kissing her on the cheek, too*)

HORACE: Well, you're almost a grown-up girl now, aren't you?

ANDREW: And such a lovely one, too.

BEAUTY: Thank you, sir.

KING: The joy of her mother's and my lives.

BEAUTY: Now, Father.

KING: But it's true.

QUEEN: She knows it is.

BEAUTY: Mother, this is going to be such a wonderful party.

May I please go and get Nanny to come, too? She's always been so good to me, and I want her to celebrate with us.

QUEEN: Well . . .

KING: Certainly you may, if that's what you want. Today you can have anything your heart desires.

BEAUTY: Thank you, Father. I'll just run up to her room and bring her down.

CURTAIN

SCENE III. A small room in the tower of the palace.
    An old woman sits at a spinning wheel spinning.

BEAUTY: (*Off stage*) Nanny! Nanny! I have a surprise for you.

BEAUTY: (*She enters.*) Oh, I must have the wrong room. I thought this was Nanny's door. Excuse me.

OLD WOMAN: Don't worry, child. You're welcome here. Come right in.

BEAUTY: Thank you. I must have made the wrong turn some-where. I felt sure that this was Nanny's room.

OLD WOMAN: Why, I'm glad you did. I've been wanting to meet you. You're the Princess, aren't you?

BEAUTY: Yes, ma'am.

OLD WOMAN: Well, come closer, so an old woman with bad eyesight can see you.

BEAUTY: All right. (*She crosses to her.*)

OLD WOMAN: My. Such a beautiful dress.

BEAUTY: Isn't it, though? It's a present from my parents for my sixteenth birthday.

OLD WOMAN: Wasn't that nice?

BEAUTY: Yes, and Mother and Father are giving me a party right now, but I wanted Nanny to come, so I came to get her.

OLD WOMAN: How thoughtful of you! Come closer so that I can see your face better.

BEAUTY: If you like.

OLD WOMAN: You must be as kind as you are beautiful.

BEAUTY: I try to be.

OLD WOMAN: I'm sure you do.

BEAUTY: What's that?

OLD WOMAN: It's a spinning wheel, dear.

BEAUTY: A spinning wheel? What's it for?

OLD WOMAN: Why it's for making thread. See I just put my foot on the pedal and the wheel turns.

BEAUTY: It looks like it would be fun to do.

OLD WOMAN: It used to be, but now it just passes the time.

BEAUTY: Is it hard?

OLD WOMAN: Not really, once you learn how.

BEAUTY: I wish I could do it.

OLD WOMAN: Why don't you then? Come here and sit in my chair. (*She rises.*)

BEAUTY: You're sure you don't mind?

OLD WOMAN: Of course not.

BEAUTY: All right then. (*She sits.*) Is this the way?

OLD WOMAN: Just right.

BEAUTY: But I can't make the wheel go around as fast as you do.

OLD WOMAN: It takes practice.

BEAUTY: What's that? (*She touches the spindle.*)

OLD WOMAN: That's the spindle.

BEAUTY: Oh, I cut my finger!

OLD WOMAN: Are you all right?

BEAUTY: I guess so. It doesn't hurt . . . much, . . . but . . . all of a sudden . . . I'm so sleepy I can hardly hold my eyes open. . . . I think I'll just close them a minute until my finger quits . . . hurting. (*She falls asleep.*)

HORTENSE: (*Entering*) Ha! Ha! I have you, my Beauty! You are mine now. Sleep, little Beauty. Sleep, and sleep, and sleep! Ha! Ha! (*She exits.*)

(*The old woman looks frightened and tries to awaken Beauty.*)

VOICES: (*Offstage*) Beauty. Beauty!

(*Nanny, now with white hair, enters followed by Jason.*)

NANNY: Beauty. We've been searching all over for you.

JASON: Yes, and when you weren't in Nanny's room we got frightened.

NANNY: Beauty. (*She crosses to her.*) Beauty. Wake up. (*She shakes Beauty.*) Jason, get the king. I can't awaken her.

JASON: Oh, no! I'll get him immediately. (*He exits.*)

NANNY: Precious, wake up. Look at Nanny. Let me see your pretty eyes . . . Beauty . . . (*She shakes her again.*) Beauty. It's all right. Speak to me, Beauty.

(*The king and the queen enter, followed by Jason. The queen rushes to Beauty. Nanny moves aside.*)

QUEEN: Darling, are you all right?

NANNY: I can't awaken her, Your Majesty. I tried and tried.

QUEEN: Oh, no. Albert, look. There's blood on her sweet little finger. She must have pricked it on this spindle.

KING: A spindle! I ordered every one in the kingdom destroyed when she was just a baby.

OLD WOMAN: But, Sir. I didn't know. I never leave my rooms.

QUEEN: Oh, Albert. I was so sure she was safe I forgot about Hortense. How could I? Oh, my poor baby! (*Crying*)

KING: I thought she was safe, too.

QUEEN: Now she'll sleep a hundred years.

KING: And she'll be all alone when she awakens. She won't know anyone.

QUEEN: Oh, poor Beauty!

ANGELA: (*Who has entered quietly and been looking on*) Would you like to sleep too for one hundred years?

KING: Of course.

QUEEN: Yes, oh, yes!

HERBERT: (*Rushing in*) Have you found her? Oh, there she is . . . asleep!

COOK: (*Entering with a hand raised to hit Herbert with a skillet*) You, ruffian. How could you leave in the middle of a party? I'll . . .

ANGELA: Then you shall have your wish. Everyone in the castle shall sleep until Beauty awakens. (*Heads drop, and actors freeze in standing positions. The cook's skillet remains in the air.*)

CURTAIN

SCENE IV. The same room one hundred years later
  The room is dark. Note: If this scene is played on a stage with an apron, the first part of the scene with Arnold and the prince may be played in front of the curtain.

ARNOLD: Wait up. After climbing all these steps I can't move another foot. That's a fine way to be treating the one who's taken care of you since you were a baby!

PRINCE: I'm sorry, Arnold. I really am.

ARNOLD: Well, you should be, putting an old man through all the things you've been making me do.

PRINCE: (*Entering, followed by Arnold*) I know, Arnold. But I really had to come.

ARNOLD: Had to come? That's the silliest thing I ever heard of.

PRINCE: It may seem that way to you.

ARNOLD: Seem? Any fool would know that it is!

PRINCE: You'll feel better after you rest a few minutes.

ARNOLD: I'll never be the same. (*He sits on the floor, takes off his shoe, and rubs his foot.*) There. That's better. I can still wiggle my toes!

PRINCE: I'm glad.

ARNOLD: Well, you should be. But look at my shoes. There's a hole in each sole. (*He holds up his shoes.*)

PRINCE: If you say so.

ARNOLD: Say so! Know so. And look at these clothes. They're totally ragged from climbing up all those thorny hedges.

PRINCE: That was a little rough.

ARNOLD: I'll say. I don't know how we ever found this place.

PRINCE: Well, we did, and now that you've had a chance to rest I'm ready to go on looking.

ARNOLD: Looking, but you can't see anything!

PRINCE: I know, but maybe I can find a window that's been closed with a shutter.

ARNOLD: Who cares? Let's just turn around and go back.

PRINCE: I can't go back. Not until we've searched every room in the palace.

ARNOLD: There couldn't possibly be anything way up here.

PRINCE: But she has to be here somewhere.

ARNOLD: Says who?

PRINCE: Everyone. I've been hearing stories about the beautiful sleeping princess all my life.

ARNOLD: Just another fairy tale.

PRINCE: We've come too far now to stop. Besides this has to be the place. There were all those people sound asleep down-stairs.

ARNOLD: That was strange.

PRINCE: The story must be true.

ARNOLD: Well, maybe so.

PRINCE: I'm going to look around for a window while you put on your shoes.

ARNOLD: All you'll find is more dust.

PRINCE: No, I won't. I've found a latch, but it won't move. It's stuck. There. (*The lights come up, and if the scene has been played on the apron the curtain is drawn.*) Arnold, look!

ARNOLD: Why there really are people up here!

PRINCE: (*Going up to Herbert and shaking him*) And I can't awaken them, either.

ARNOLD: Hey, look at this one with the frying pan. Does this one ever look mad! Probably feels about like I do!

PRINCE: (*Wandering around*) Arnold!

ARNOLD: Yes.

PRINCE: Come over here. I think I've found the king and queen!

ARNOLD: (*Walks to them and looks them over*) You could be right. They're wearing crowns!

PRINCE: And look. There's a girl over there by the spinning wheel.

ARNOLD: Do you think she could be the one we've been looking for?

PRINCE: (*Going to her*) Arnold, she has to be. Look she's wearing a little crown, and she's beautiful!

ARNOLD: She is kind of pretty.

PRINCE: Kind of! She's gorgeous. She must be the one we've heard so much about.

ARNOLD: And if she's not, do we still have to keep going?

PRINCE: This has to be her. (*He touches her hair, then her face.*) Beauty. Beauty. Wake up!

ARNOLD: (*Moving closer*) I think she moved.

PRINCE: Beauty . . . Beauty. It's all right. We're here to help you. Wake up, Beauty.

BEAUTY: (*Moves her head, opens her eyes, and slowly stretches.*) I must have taken a little nap.

ARNOLD: I'll say! (*The king, queen, cook, Herbert, and old woman slowly start to open their eyes and move.*)

PRINCE: You've been asleep quite a long time.

BEAUTY: I have?

PRINCE: Yes.

QUEEN: Oh, darling, you're awake!

KING: And we are, too. But who are you?

PRINCE: I'm Prince Phillip of the kingdom in the south.

KING: But there's no Prince Phillip there. King Frederick's son is called Alex.

PRINCE: You must be talking about my great grandfather.

KING: Great grandfather?

PRINCE: Yes, he lived a hundred years ago, during the time everyone in this castle went to sleep.

BEAUTY: A hundred years!

KING: Of course. I should have remembered.

QUEEN: The good fairy Angela did make everything work out right! I've never been so happy.

BEAUTY: But I don't understand.

PRINCE: I've been hearing the stories about you ever since I was a little boy. The legend said you would keep sleeping until a prince who cared about you very much came and awakened you.

BEAUTY: And you really care about me?

ARNOLD: I'll say!

PRINCE: Enough to journey far in search of you. Do you think you could learn to care for me, too?

BEAUTY: How could you not be special when you've done so much for me?

KING: Good. Then it's settled.

QUEEN: And we must have a feast to celebrate. Cook, go right down to the kitchen and see what you can find for us to eat.

KING: Good. I'm starving!

COOK: Of course, Your Highness. And you . . . (*Raises the skillet and goes toward Herbert, who starts to run*) This time you're not going to sneak away like you're always doing. This time you're going to stay and do the work you're supposed to be doing.

(*The others smile and look at each other.*)

HERBERT: Oh, I will. I will . . . when you catch me!

CURTAIN

THE MAGIC POT

Cast of Characters

Andrew, a mover
Robert, a mover
The Foreman
Father
Lawrence, his son
Mr. Pennypincher
Arnold, his bookkeeper
The Stranger
Frank, the butler
Jane, a maid
Cook

Mother
Jill, her daughter
Jennifer, a daughter
Bettina, a daughter
Lola, a friend
Vertna, a friend
Hazel, a friend
The Pot
Mrs. Pennypincher
Alice, a maid

Production Notes

The *Magic Pot* was written for nine boys and twelve girls. If
fewer boys' parts are needed, the foreman, Arnold, and Frank may

be played by one person or two. To add more boys have The Pot played by a boy; change Vertna and Hazel's roles to men's parts, or have boys come with Lola, Vertna, and Hazel as their husbands. To have fewer girls Jane, Alice, and the Cook can also be played by Vertna, Lola, and Hazel. Cook may be a boy or girl. Other girls may come with Vertna, Lola, and Hazel as walk-ons, or their lines may be divided between them.

Discussion Questions

Use the following for discussion or as topics for creative writing.

1. We tend to think that a person can always *do* something to better a situation, but in many cultural situations the individuals cannot. Does a belief in magic help? Does it prevent people from doing something to change things?
2. Was it smart for Lawrence to sell the cow, Moo Moo? He would get money, but the family would lose their milk from the cow.
3. Do you think it was important for Lawrence to be so concerned about finding a good home for the cow instead of just seeing how much money he could get? Was he perhaps rewarded for this considerate attitude by getting the magic pot?
4. Was it smart for Lawrence to trust the man who wanted to trade the pot for the cow? The last time the family trusted someone, Mr. Pennypincher, they got cheated. The second time things worked out. How can you tell when to trust somebody?
5. Do you think the Father should have been more cautious when he made the bargain with Mr. Pennypincher? Was it unwise to have done business with him since he was known to cheat people?
6. If you find yourself in a very unfair situation with people having power over you, what can you do?

7. Why didn't the Schmidts' neighbors help them out when they were in so much trouble? Should we help our friends and neighbors?

8. Bettina tried to make the family laugh and feel better about their situation. How can family members contribute to each other's good feelings? What has your family done to make you feel good about yourself?

9. What do you never want to do in your own family when you grow up?

10. Write a story about someone whose family helps them a great deal, or whose family makes life harder for them.

11. Why is being responsible so important in a family? What does everyone need to get from a family?

Enrichment Activities

Suggestions for the teacher. The Magic Pot is a Danish fairy tale. Setting the play in Denmark gives the students the opportunity of familiarizing themselves with this section of Scandinavia. Have students do an activity from at least one category and teach the others in the class what they have learned. Children may work individually or in groups to complete assignments.

Select one of the following projects to do:

1. Enlarge a map of Denmark and put it on poster or butcher paper. Using an opaque or overhead projector for which a transparency has been made, will facilitate the project.

2. Tell the story of the play in pictures. Put the illustrations on wallpaper or newsprint. You can then make a television box by cutting off the folding parts of a corrugated box and making holes in the top for dowels. Make the dowels slightly higher than the box and attach the paper with the pictures in series. A movie can then be shown by placing the illustrations toward the front of the box and rolling the picture from one side to the other.

3. Dress a doll in traditional Danish clothing.
4. Make a scene from the play from modeling clay.
5. Make box scenes for the play. To do this cut off one side of a corrugated box and decorate the inside to represent one of the scenes of the play. Make paper doll figures to represent the characters of the play and hold them in place with lumps of clay. People may be dressed from scraps of paper or fabric and mounted on paste sticks or straws.
6. Make a model of a Viking ship.
7. Make a large picture of a Viking.

Write a report on one of the following:

1. Denmark. Include information on the following: the capital, climate, principal crops, manufacturing, fishing, and exports.
2. The Vikings
3. Scandinavia
4. Hans Christian Andersen
5. Eric the Red
6. Leif Ericson
7. Iceland

Do one of the following activities:

1. Write a character description of Lawrence.
2. Write a character description of Mr. Pennypincher.
3. Write a character description of Mrs. Pennypincher.
4. Write a news release for the play *The Magic Pot*.
5. Write an imaginary interview with The Pot.

The Magic Pot—Play Script

SCENE I. The home of the Schmidts, a poor family.
The Schmidts and their four children, Jill, Jennifer, Bettina, and

Lawrence, watch as the foreman and his two helpers, Andrew and Robert, carry the family furniture out of the house.

ROBERT: I guess this chair goes? (*Pointing to a chair*)

FOREMAN: That's right.

ANDREW: What about the one over there? (*Pointing to another chair*)

FOREMAN: I'm afraid so. (*Robert and Andrew exit carrying the chairs.*)

JILL: Father, how can you just stand there and let them take away our furniture?

FATHER: I don't have any choice. We have to eat.

JENNIFER: But they've already taken our beds, our tables, and our other chairs.

FATHER: I know.

BETTINA: Well, you don't want to sit on a chair and put your plate on the floor when you eat, do you?

JILL: Of course, I don't.

BETTINA: Then what's so important about the chairs?

JILL: If you don't know I'm just not going to tell you.

MOTHER: She knows. She's trying to help. Aren't you, Bettina?

LAWRENCE: If you really want to help you could go with them to put things on the wagon so we'll get our money sooner.

FATHER: That's enough of that. Everything will be all right.

JILL: But, Father, they're taking away everything we own.

BETTINA: Not quite everything. We've still got our clothes on.

JILL: Oh, Bettina.

MOTHER: And we've got our health.

FATHER: And selling this is going to give us money to buy some food so we can eat.

JENNIFER: That's good.

JILL: I know. I'm hungry.

MOTHER: Hush, Jill. As soon as Mr. Pennypincher lets us have our food I'll fix us something to eat.

LAWRENCE: I'm starved. . . . We haven't eaten anything since yesterday.

FOREMAN: I know, and I'm really sorry. Not having work is bad, but money from your furniture will help.

FATHER: I'm counting on it.

FOREMAN: I wish I were the one to decide how much you'll get for everything.

FATHER: I do, too. I know you'd be fair.

FOREMAN: I would be, too. (*Andrew and Robert enter.*)

ANDREW: Do we have everything now? (*Looking around the empty room*)

FATHER: Yes, that does it.

ROBERT: I'll tell Mr. Pennypincher, then. (*Robert and Andrew exit.*)

FOREMAN: (*Shaking Father's hand*) I'm sorry. (*He exits.*)

MOTHER: I do hope he'll give us enough money to buy food until you get work again.

JILL: We do, too.

MOTHER: Hush.

FATHER: All we can do is hope.

MOTHER: Well, I've heard that he always cheats people!

FATHER: Maybe he won't cheat us.

MOTHER: I hope not.

(*Mr. Pennypincher enters followed by Arnold, the accountant, who is busily writing figures into a notebook.*)

MR. PENNYPINCHER: We have everything now, I understand.

FATHER: That's right.

MR. PENNYPINCHER: You are certainly fortunate to have me take this old junk off your hands and give you some food for it, too.

MOTHER: We're all hungry. We need money.

LAWRENCE: We're almost starving.

MR. PENNYPINCHER: This certainly is your lucky day, then. I had heard you were in need of food so we brought some out to you in the wagon when we came.

FATHER: That's very good of you, sir.

MR. PENNYPINCHER: It certainly is. I'm glad you realize it.

FATHER: Oh, we do, sir.

MR. PENNYPINCHER: Of course, I'm really very disappointed in the junk you have for me in exchange. It's worthless.

MOTHER: But we gave you everything we had.

MR. PENNYPINCHER: Which is hardly equal to the generous amounts of food I brought to you. Is it, Arnold?

ARNOLD: (*Shaking his head, no.*) Not at the prices you say, sir.

MR. PENNYPINCHER: You see?

FATHER: Yes.

MR. PENNYPINCHER: If it weren't for me and my generosity you'd only have half as much as I'm giving you.

FATHER: Thank you, sir. We appreciate all you're doing for us.

MR. PENNYPINCHER: Arnold.

ARNOLD: Yes, sir.

MR. PENNYPINCHER: Go tell Robert and Andrew to bring in the groceries we brought.

ARNOLD: Yes, sir. (*He exits.*)

MR. PENNYPINCHER: You seem to have a fine family here.

FATHER: That we do.

MR. PENNYPINCHER: What are your names?

BETTINA: I'm Bettina, Mr. Pennypincher. (*She curtsies.*)

JENNIFER: And I'm Jennifer, sir. (*Curtsying*)

JILL: My name is Jill. (*She curtsies.*)

(*Mr. Pennypincher turns to Lawrence, who is staring vacantly into space.*)

MR. PENNYPINCHER: And you, young man?

(*Bettina kicks Lawrence to get his attention.*)

MR. PENNYPINCHER: And you, young man.

LAWRENCE: I'm Lawrence, sir.

MR. PENNYPINCHER: You have a fine family here.

FATHER: Yes, sir, but we need money to live on, and I must have a job. Don't you have something I could do?

MR. PENNYPINCHER: No, I'm afraid not.

FATHER: But, sir, I'd work very hard.

MR. PENNYPINCHER: No. I can't use you.

(*Andrew and Robert enter carrying two large cloth sacks that appear to be full. They set them down.*)

ANDREW: This is it, sir.

MR. PENNYPINCHER: Fine, then we can be going. I've wasted enough of my time on a good deed for today. Here's your money.

(*Pennypincher, Andrew, and Robert exit.*)

LAWRENCE: Good, they're gone. Now we can get something to eat. (*He starts looking into one of the bags. The girls go to the other one and start rummaging through, too.*)

JILL: MO . . . O . . . O . . . THER! (*Screaming!*) MOTHER!

MOTHER: Yes, what is it?

JENNIFER: The vegetables are only on top, see? (*She holds up a potato.*) There are only eight of these in the bag!

MOTHER: (*Crossing to them*) I don't understand.

BETTINA: Look what's underneath. (*The others peer into the bag.*)

JILL: The bottom of the bag is filled with rocks!

JENNIFER: Rocks, Mother!

BETTINA: Maybe he thinks we like stone soup!

JILL: Oh, Bettina!

JENNIFER: How could you try to be funny at a time like this?

MOTHER: He's cheated us! I knew he would. What about the money?

FATHER: (*Counting it*) There's not much, but what could I do?

MOTHER: I know what you CAN do.

FATHER: What?

MOTHER: Go after him. Talk to him.

FATHER: It wouldn't do any good. You know that.

MOTHER: You can try.

FATHER: But you saw him. You know how he is.

MOTHER: Look here. We gave away all our furniture in order to have only about three good meals!

JILL: And then we'll be hungry again!

JENNIFER: Oooooh!

LAWRENCE: And I'm a growing boy. I need to eat lots.

FATHER: All right, I'll go.

MOTHER: You'd better.

FATHER: But don't expect it to do any good! (*He exits.*)

JILL: I bet it won't either!

JENNIFER: We're going to starve!

MOTHER: No, we'll think of something.

BETTINA: We'll have to, soon. This food won't last long.

MOTHER: That's true.

LAWRENCE: Mother, I have an idea.

MOTHER: What is it?

JENNIFER: A good one?

LAWRENCE: Yes, while father's gone, I'll take the cow and go sell her to somebody.

MOTHER: But who would you sell her to?

LAWRENCE: I don't know, but I'll find somebody besides mean old Mr. Pennypincher.

BETTINA: Oh, but poor Moo Moo.

JILL: Silly, she's just a cow.

BETTINA: But she's been so good to us.

MOTHER: Well, maybe the new owners can give her more to eat.

BETTINA: That's true.

JENNIFER: Yes. Hurry now, Lawrence, before Father gets back.

JILL: He'll never let you go.

MOTHER: I think they're right. It's our only chance.

LAWRENCE: All right. I'll leave now.

JENNIFER: Get lots of money.

LAWRENCE: I'll try. (*He exits.*)

BETTINA: Poor Moo Moo. I should have gone to tell her good-bye.

JILL: How could a cow know the difference?

BETTINA: Moo Moo would!

MOTHER: Maybe it's just as well. Telling her good-bye could have just made her sad.

BETTINA: You're probably right.

JILL: Mother, may I have an apple now? I'm terribly hungry.

MOTHER: I know you are, but why don't you and Bettina and Jennifer divide one instead?

JILL: But that's hardly any.

MOTHER: Then chew it slowly to make it last.

JENNIFER: Oh, mother.

(*There is a knock on the door.*)

BETTINA: I'll go.

(*Three peasant women enter. They look around the room.*)

LOLA: Oh, you poor dears!

VERTNA: They took away all of your furniture.

HAZEL: Do you even have beds?

JILL: No, there's nothing left at all. It's terrible.

MOTHER: It's not good.

LOLA: You must be heartbroken.

MOTHER: We all are.

HAZEL: Did you get a good price for your things?

JENNIFER: No. Father almost gave them away!

BETTINA: Jennifer, he couldn't help it. He did the best he could.

JILL: He could have at least looked to see that these two bags were filled with food.

BETTINA: None of us thought of it either.

LOLA: You mean they're not full?

JILL: No. Only the tops have anything to eat.

JENNIFER: The bottoms of the bags are filled with rocks!

HAZEL: Oh, that's terrible!

VERTNA: I knew Mr. Pennypincher was mean but I didn't know he was THAT mean!

LOLA: I told you not to trust him.

MOTHER: I know, but what could we do?

JILL: Father's gone to talk to him now, but I know it won't do any good!

JENNIFER: And Lawrence has gone to try to sell Moo Moo. That's all we have left.

HAZEL: Oh, you poor things.

VERTNA Yes, it's a sad day.

LOLA: A sad day, indeed. (*Shaking her head.*)

CURTAIN

SCENE II. The road to town.
   (*Lawrence enters and stops and looks back over his shoulder, calling to the cow.*)

LAWRENCE: Moo Moo, you just stop and eat some grass. I know you're hungry and tired. . . . That's the way, you rest a little while. . . . Poor Moo Moo . . . and such a good girl. I'll bet that tastes good to you, poor thing. You haven't had a real meal in weeks.

STRANGER: Hello, there. (*Entering*)

LAWRENCE: Hi!

STRANGER: Hot day for walking, isn't it? (*He mops his forehead with a handkerchief he's taken out of his pocket.*)

LAWRENCE: Sure is. Poor Moo Moo got mighty tired. That's why I'm stopping to let her rest awhile.

STRANGER: Moo Moo that cow over there?

LAWRENCE: Yeah, but she's really more than that to us. She's a pet, too.

STRANGER: Why do you have her out of her shed on such a hot day, then?

LAWRENCE: I'm taking her into town to see if I can sell her.

STRANGER: You must hate to do that since she's your pet.

LAWRENCE: Yes, but I have to. I have to get some money for the family, and besides we're so poor now we can't afford to feed her any more.

STRANGER: That's too bad. Sounds like times are pretty bad.

LAWRENCE: Yeah. I sure hope I can find someone who'll care about her the way we do.

STRANGER: She must be a very special cow.

LAWRENCE: Oh, she is. She understands everything you say to her.

STRANGER: I'd sure like to have a cow like that.

LAWRENCE: You can get her for a mighty good price.

STRANGER: That's the problem. I'm hard up for money, too, right now.

LAWRENCE: Too bad, I'd like to see you have her. You look like the sort of man who would be kind to her.

STRANGER: Oh, I would be. . . . Say, I do have something I could give you in exchange but it's not money.

LAWRENCE: What is it?

STRANGER: It's right over there. I'll bring it over here so you can see for yourself.

LAWRENCE: All right.

(*The stranger exits briefly, then returns with a child dressed as a pot, walking on its knees.*)

STRANGER: I'll give you this for Moo Moo.

LAWRENCE: That old pot!

STRANGER: Yes, but it's not just what it seems.

POT: No, I'm a very special pot, and you're going to like me a lot.

LAWRENCE: (*Scratching his head*) I thought I heard it say something.

POT: Oh, you did!

LAWRENCE I did? But that's not possible.

POT: Who says it's not? I'm a talking pot.

LAWRENCE: That's certainly different!

STRANGER: I told you it wasn't what it seems. Do we have a deal?

LAWRENCE: I'd like to take it, but I can't. I need money. My family is hungry and old Mr. Pennypincher just cheated us out of all our furniture. This is all we have left to sell.

POT: Take me! Take me. You'll be glad if you do. I'll see that there's food for your family and you.

LAWRENCE: You really mean it? You can do that?

STRANGER: It means it. It can help you.

LAWRENCE: I don't know.

POT: Take me. Please, take me. You'll really soon see . . . how very much better I'll make all things be.

LAWRENCE: Well . . . I don't know . . . Maybe . . .

STRANGER: Then we'll trade?

LAWRENCE: Yes . . . yes, I'll do it. Moo Moo is yours.

CURTAIN

SCENE III. The Schmidts' Cottage.
   (*Jill and Jennifer sit on the floor reading. Mother sweeps. Bettina enters.*)

BETTINA: I just went out to Moo Moo's stall. It's sad with her gone.

MOTHER: And mad is what your father's going to be. He really loved that old cow.

BETTINA: That's why Lawrence had to be the one to try to sell her. Father couldn't have done it.

MOTHER: And we had to have some money. (*Lawrence enters.*)

MOTHER: You're already back!

BETTINA Did you sell Moo Moo?

LAWRENCE: Yes.

MOTHER: Wonderful.

JILL: (*Rising*) Good. Now we'll have lots of money to buy food, and maybe buy back our furniture.

LAWRENCE: Well . . .

JENNIFER: (*Putting her book down and rising*) How much did you get?

MOTHER: It better be a lot. We need every cent we can get.

BETTINA: Do you think that the people who bought her will be good to Moo Moo?

LAWRENCE: Oh, yes.

MOTHER: Fine. Now let's count the money. Give it to me.

LAWRENCE: Uh . . . I don't have any money.

MOTHER: You don't have Moo Moo OR any money?

LAWRENCE: That's right.

BETTINA: You're teasing, aren't you? (*Lawrence shakes his head no.*)

JILL: How could you have done this to us?

JENNIFER: He's stupid, that's how.

MOTHER: Oh, Lawrence, I trusted you. What will your father say?

LAWRENCE: He'll be happy. That's what.

MOTHER: Happy?

LAWRENCE: Yes. Wait till you see what I got in exchange.

JENNIFER: And what was that?

LAWRENCE: A pot.

JILL: A POT?

MOTHER: I can't believe it!

BETTINA: Maybe he's gone without food for so long it's affected his mind.

LAWRENCE: (*Exiting*) This pot's different. You'll see. (*Returning with the pot*)

JILL: It doesn't look different to me. It's just older and uglier.

JENNIFER: And we won't even have food to put in it.

POT: But I came here to help you. You'll really soon see . . . how very much better I'll make things to be.

BETTINA: I thought it said something.

JILL: Silly, a pot can't talk.

MOTHER: But I heard it, too.

POT: Now, ladies, be careful and please don't you fight. I already know which one of you's right.

BETTINA: We did hear him!

JENNIFER: How could we?

POT: Because it's true. I talked to you.

MOTHER: It can talk!

POT: Yes. I came to tell you to worry no more. Things'll be better than they've been before. I'm leaving now, but I'll soon be back. And I'm gonna bring you some things that you lack.

LAWRENCE: Where are you going?

POT: To the Pennypinchers is where I'll go. And just what I'll get there you'll very soon know. (*The Pot starts to leave.*)

LAWRENCE: But Pot . . .

POT: By noon I'll be back with things that you lack.

CURTAIN

SCENE IV. The road to the Pennypincher's.
  (*On a proscenium stage this scene can take place in front of the act curtain. The Pot enters followed by the Stranger.*)

STRANGER: Hey, Little Pot. Wait!

POT: But I've got work to do. I've others to help now besides only you.

STRANGER: How's everything going?

POT: Fine. They're soon gonna see. How very much better I'll make all things be.

STRANGER: Oh?

POT: Yes, I'm on my way, and soon at the Pennypinchers I'll have my say.

STRANGER: That should be interesting.

POT: Yes, he's gonna learn that we are all brothers, and that it doesn't pay when we start to cheat others.

STRANGER: Good. That's a lesson he should have learned a long time ago.

POT: But since that he didn't, I'm making a vow. He's soon gonna learn it, and learn it right now!

CURTAIN

SCENE V. The Pennypinchers' kitchen.
   (The Pot, Mrs. Pennypincher, and servants are on stage.)

MRS. PENNYPINCHER: You do understand that tonight is very important to me, don't you?

BUTLER: Yes, madam.

MRS. PENNYPINCHER: Only the very best people will be here.

JANE: Oh, naturally, ma'am.

MRS. PENNYPINCHER: People who are used to the finest of foods and homes.

ALICE: Certainly, ma'am. We know your friends are all very rich.

MRS. PENNYPINCHER: So you simply must do your best in every way.

BUTLER: You can depend on it, madam.

MRS. PENNYPINCHER: And that goes for the food, too, Cook.

COOK: Of course, Mrs. Pennypincher.

MRS. PENNYPINCHER: I expect you to serve the most delicious meal of your lives. Do you understand?

COOK: Certainly, Mrs. Pennypincher. You can depend on me.

MRS. PENNYPINCHER: I want only the freshest of vegetables.

COOK: Of course.

MRS. PENNYPINCHER: And the tenderest of meats.

COOK: The best money can buy.

MRS. PENNYPINCHER: And you, Alice and Jane, do you understand that you are to work with Cook in the kitchen preparing the meal, then help Frank out in the dining room when the guests arrive?

JANE: We understand, Mrs. Pennypincher, don't we Alice? (*She nudges her.*)

ALICE: Oh certainly, ma'am.

MRS. PENNYPINCHER: Very good. Remember I am depending on you to make this the most elegant, elaborate, expensive meal that's ever been served anywhere in these parts.

BUTLER: It will be, madam, and we will serve it perfectly.

MRS. PENNYPINCHER: See that you do, Frank. (*She exits.*)

(*Jane runs after her and makes a face behind her back.*)

JANE: (*Turning and mocking Mrs. Pennypincher*) You do understand don't you, that only the best is good enough for our friends!

ALICE: As if they deserved it any more than anyone else!

COOK: Makes me sick to think of them stuffing themselves with all this good food, and most people without enough to eat!

BUTLER: True, but we'd better get busy or we won't have jobs and we'll be hungry, too.

COOK: Well, this pot roast's ready. (*Crossing to the Pot*)

JANE: (*Mocking Mrs. Pennypincher*) Does it have only the tenderest of meat and the freshest of vegetables?

COOK: Just as she ordered. Come taste it yourselves. (*Takes a long stirring spoon from an apron pocket and holds it out to them*)

BUTLER: I'll take your word for it.

JANE: It's good. I sampled it a while ago.

ALICE: Well, I'd like some. (*She takes the spoon from the Cook's hand, goes to the Pot and pretends to stir the food, then she tastes it.*) This is wonderful!

COOK: Too good for them.

ALICE: And look how much you've made.

JANE: (*Crossing to look in the Pot*) Why there's enough in here to feed a family of six for a whole month!

POT: And I'm here to tell you, that's just what I'll do.

COOK: That pot is talking!

ALICE: And it's moving.

POT: And going with all your good chow. And you'll never catch me, I'm telling you now.

BUTLER: I can't believe it!

JANE: (*Laughing*) And I can't either. Serves her right.

ALICE: Won't it be funny for them to be hungry for a change!

BUTLER: They can find out what it's like to skip a meal.

JANE: For once! Some of them need to do it lots of times.

ALICE: They're not going to like it a bit.

COOK: But she'll think we did it on purpose.

ALICE: She will!

(*They rush to the door.*)

JANE: We've got to get that pot back!

BUTLER: Yes! (*He rushes out the door, then hurries back.*) I can't see it anywhere. The Pot is gone! (*Others are dismayed*)

CURTAIN

SCENE VI. The Schmidts' cottage.
  (*The Schmidt family is sitting on the floor talking to the Pot.*)

BETTINA: That's the best meal I've ever eaten.

LAWRENCE: And I can't ever remember having so much good food.

MOTHER: It seems like the more we eat, the more there is, too. Every pot, pan, and bowl we have is still filled.

POT: I told you I'd take care of you. Now you saw I did it, too.

FATHER: That you did. Lawrence, I'm sorry for all the things I said to you about trading Moo Moo for the Pot.

LAWRENCE: Thank you, Father.

POT: Now don't you see that you can trust me?

JILL: I do.

JENNIFER: And I do, too.

BETTINA: It would be hard not to after this meal.

POT: And soon you will see that the best is yet to be.

MOTHER: There's more?

POT: You bet there'll be more. Good things are in store.

FATHER: But I don't see how.

POT: But soon now you will, for this pot I will fill.

JENNIFER: You're leaving? Where are you going?

POT: If you have to know, to the rich man's house is just where I'll go.

JILL: The rich man's house! Are you talking about Mr. Pennypincher?

POT: I guess I'll confess, that's a pretty good guess.

BETTINA: Well, good luck, Little Pot. We don't know how to thank you as it is.

(*The Pot starts to exit and then turns.*)

POT: Just watching you eat and seeing your smiles will keep me going for miles and for miles. (*Pot exits.*)

OTHERS: Good-bye, Little Pot. Hurry back.

CURTAIN

SCENE VII. Mr. Pennypincher's house.
   Mr. Pennypincher and the butler are on stage. There is a table with several cloth bags on it. The Pot and a chair are next to it.

MR. PENNYPINCHER: I am not to be disturbed. Is that understood?

BUTLER: Yes, sir.

MR. PENNYPINCHER: Under no circumstances whatsoever.

BUTLER: As you wish, sir.

MR. PENNYPINCHER: Very good. You may go.

BUTLER: Thank you, sir. (*He exits.*)

(*Mr. Pennypincher goes to the table and sits in the chair beside it. Next he opens a bag which is full of coins. He dumps them on the table and gleefully starts to count them.*)

MR. PENNYPINCHER: Ah, my beautiful money . . . Look at you shining there. And you're mine. I can have everything I want. EVERYTHING! Wonderful, wonderful money! I love to look at you. I love to feel you! I love to count you! Let me see. One, two, three, four, five. (*He puts the coins in a stack, then he stacks others in groups of five.*) Ten . . . fifteen . . . twenty. (*There is a knock on the door.*)

MR. PENNYPINCHER: Go away. Don't bother me.

ALICE: But, Mr. Pennypincher, I must see you.

MR. PENNYPINCHER: Didn't you hear me?

ALICE: Yes, sir, but it's important, sir. Please let me in.

(*Mr. Pennypincher looks around for some place to put the money. He sees the Pot and piles the money inside, then he goes to the door.*)

MR. PENNYPINCHER: This had better be important.

ALICE: Oh, it is, sir. (*She enters.*) I assure you. It's Mrs. Pennypincher, sir.

MR. PENNYPINCHER: What about Mrs. Pennypincher?

ALICE: Well, you know how unhappy she was about that pot running away and taking all the food for the party.

MR. PENNYPINCHER: And having to send all of our guests away hungry. Of course, she was unhappy! Unhappy and embarrassed! Who wouldn't be?

ALICE: Anybody would be, sir. I understand, sir.

MR. PENNYPINCHER: You came here just to tell me that?

ALICE: Oh no, sir. I came to tell you that now Mrs. Pennypincher has taken to her bed and refuses to eat or go out.

MR. PENNYPINCHER: So what?

ALICE: So we were worried. We thought you would be, too, sir, and that you'd want to go up and talk to her and try to make her feel better.

MR. PENNYPINCHER: What do I care about her? That's what she gets for hiring someone as stupid as that cook! She deserves to be sent away without any money for doing that. She made us look ridiculous.

ALICE: But, Mr. Pennypincher, sir, Cook just thought it was a regular household pot. Nobody could have told the difference.

MR. PENNYPINCHER: I would certainly think that anyone with any intelligence would be able to. I'm sure I could.

ALICE: But . . .

MR. PENNYPINCHER: Enough. I'm busy. Get out of here at once, and leave me alone.

ALICE: All right, sir. (*She exits.*) I'm sorry, sir. I thought . . .

MR. PENNYPINCHER: You obviously can't think! . . . Now back to my beautiful gold. (*He crosses to the Pot and starts to take his gold out, but it doesn't move.*)

MR. PENNYPINCHER: What's the matter with this? I can't get my gold out! (*Tugging on the gold*)

POT: And there's really quite a lot. What a shame some silly person put it all inside a pot.

MR. PENNYPINCHER: Why you said something!

POT: That I did. And I'm talking about the gold that you hid.

MR. PENNYPINCHER: But a pot can't talk!

POT: Who said that's so? I'm different. I'm magic. Or didn't you know?

MR. PENNYPINCHER: Get out of here!

POT: Gladly, sir, you'll be happy to know. But first you must tell me where you'd like me to go.

MR. PENNYPINCHER: The further the better. As far as possible. To the North Pole. Yes, that should do it.

POT: Just as you say. I'm now on my way. (*The Pot starts to exit.*)

MR. PENNYPINCHER: But not with my money. (*He runs after the Pot and grabs hold of it.*) Wait. Wait! Let me get my money out first.

POT: YOUR money, sir? This is money you took! Everyone knows you are just an old crook.

MR. PENNYPINCHER: Why I'll break you apart with my own two hands. (*He grabs hold of the Pot.*) I'll make you sorry. I'll . . . I'll . . . I can't get my hands loose. Let go of me!

POT: No. I've got you now and I want you to know, I'm taking you with me wherever I go.

MR. PENNYPINCHER: What? Why would you do that?

POT: Because of all that money you stole. You're off with me to the cold North Pole!

CURTAIN

SCENE VIII. The Schmidts' cottage.
   The Schmidt family is sitting on the floor talking.

LAWRENCE: I wonder what our Little Pot is doing now.

BETTINA: You can't ever tell with it.

JILL: It said it would be back soon. I can't wait to see what it will bring this time.

MOTHER: Now, Jill, it's done enough for us already.

JENNIFER: But mother, who knows, maybe it will do more. Besides, we need lots more things than just food.

JILL: Like beds, and tables, and chairs.

(*There is a knock outside and a voice starts to yell.*)

POT: I'm back. I'm back. Please open the door. There's someone here with more treats in store.

(Lawrence jumps up and runs to the door. The others all stand excitedly. The Pot and Mr. Pennypincher enter.)

MR. PENNYPINCHER: It's about time you stopped for a minute. I'm all tired out!

POT: But not nearly as tired, I want you to know, as you're gonna be when we get where we'll go!

LAWRENCE: Where are you going?

POT: Because of the money that he plainly stole, I'm taking him now to the far, far North Pole.

BETTINA: The North Pole!

POT: Yes, that's where he said that he thought I should be, but I'm taking him with me, as you will soon see.

MR. PENNYPINCHER: And I don't want to go!

JILL: Then why don't you turn loose and let the Pot go without you?

MR. PENNYPINCHER: I can't. It's put a spell on me.

POT: For the way that he treated all that we know, he's going with me, to see lots of snow.

JILL: Wonderful! Good riddance.

MR. PENNYPINCHER: No . . .

POT: Before I shall leave come see what I took, and have here inside me, for you, from this crook!

(*The Schmidts rush to the Pot excitedly. Father and Mother start to take out the bags of money.*)

JILL: What's in the bags?

LAWRENCE: Let me see. (*He takes a bag and opens it.*) MONEY!

(*They all look at it.*)

JENNIFER: It IS money?

MOTHER: And it's for us?

POT: That's true. There's enough for you and the others he's robbed, too.

FATHER: Good. We can give it back to them.

MR. PENNYPINCHER: And tell them I'm sorry.

BETTINA: You, sorry?

MR. PENNYPINCHER: Yes, I see that money's not the only thing that's important.

MOTHER: No. But it means a lot when you don't have any.

JILL: Like you almost left us!

MR. PENNYPINCHER: I know. I wish I had treated you better.

POT: Well, we must be going. Have to get to where it's snowing.

FATHER: Little Pot, we're grateful for all you've done.

MOTHER: And we thank you.

JENNIFER: And we'll never forget you. Or you, Mr. Penny-pincher.

MR. PENNYPINCHER: Oh, please, Little Pot. Let me stay. I'll change, I promise. I'll make it up to the ones I hurt.

POT: A chance we might try, 'cept we know how you lie.

BETTINA: But I think he means it.

LAWRENCE: I do, too.

BETTINA: Couldn't you try him a while and see how he does?

MOTHER: And if he hasn't changed, take him then?

POT: If you want to see, then it's all right with me.

LAWRENCE: Good. Then you can stay here with us, too. I'd hate to have you go, Little Pot.

POT: And as you can see, here's the place I'd rather be.

FATHER: Good. Then it's settled. We'll give Pennypincher his chance.

MR. PENNYPINCHER: And every day I'll make you glad you did.

BETTINA: I think you will.

LAWRENCE: And we're all going to live happily ever after, just like in fairy tales!

CURTAIN

SNOW WHITE AND THE SEVEN DWARFS

Cast of Characters

Herman, the Queen's servant
Huntsman, the gamekeeper
Dwarf #1, a miner
Dwarf #2, a miner
Dwarf #3, a miner

Dwarf #4, a miner
Dwarf #5, a miner
Dwarf #6, a miner
Dwarf #7, a miner
Page, Ivan's attendant
Ivan, the prince

Dorothy, a cleaning woman
Mary, a cleaning woman
Beth, a cleaning woman
Snow White, a poor princess
Queen Alexandra, Snow
 White's mean stepmother
The Mirror, a sprite
Queen Rebecca, Ivan's
 mother
Merritt, her attendant

Production Notes

Snow White was written for eleven boys and eight girls. Girls can play the parts of dwarfs. More attendants can be added in walk-on parts. Scenes II and IV can be played on the apron of the stage if traditional staging is being used. Any dances are acceptable.

Discussion Questions

The following may be used for discussion or as topics for creative writing.

1. The Queen felt that being beautiful was of prime importance. How necessary are good looks? How do they help? How can they be a handicap?
2. Which do you consider the most important: being attractive, having a good personality, or being a good person? Why?
3. What would you have done if you were the Huntsman?
4. The Queen tried to make Snow White feel bad about herself. Tell about a time when someone made you feel most confident about yourself, or a time when you felt bad about yourself.
5. What can you do to make others feel better about themselves?
6. The dwarfs were different because they were smaller. What do you think it would be like to be a grown person who was the size of a child in kindergarten? How would this be a problem?
7. In what ways are people alike and different? Write a story about someone who is different from you.
8. Snow White and the dwarfs became very good friends. What does friendship mean to you? What kinds of things do you do for your friends? What do your friends do for you?
9. What can destroy a friendship? Have you ever gotten angry with a friend or someone you loved? Why? What did you do? What happened to your friendship? Write a story about friendship.
10. How does it feel when a friend or someone you love is angry with you? What do you want to happen? What can you do to make it happen?

Enrichment Activities

Suggestions for the teacher. For research purposes set the play in England between the years 1558 and 1603, during the reign of Queen Elizabeth I. Have students do an activity from at least one category and teach the class what they have learned. Assignments may be completed by students working individually or in groups.

Select one of the following projects to do:

1. Make an accordion fold of pictures illustrating scenes of the play in sequence. Pictures should be mounted on cardboard and taped together.
2. Make a model of an Elizabethan theatre.
3. Using an overhead or opaque projector make a large map of the British Isles. Put the map on poster board or butcher paper.
4. Make illustrations of clothing worn in England during the reign of Queen Elizabeth I.
5. Dress a doll in a costume of the period.
6. Make a model of a thatched-roof English cottage.

Write a report on one of the following:

1. The climate, principal crops, manufactured items, and recreation in England.
2. Queen Elizabeth I
3. Sir Francis Drake
4. Mary, Queen of Scots
5. William Shakespeare
6. Make a time line of at least ten events that took place during the reign of Queen Elizabeth I.
7. Stonehenge. Make illustrations.
8. Sir Walter Raleigh
9. King Phillip II and the Spanish Armada
10. Henry VIII

Snow White and the Seven Dwarfs—Play Script

SCENE I. The Queen's quarters in the palace.
  Three maids are busily cleaning the room.

DOROTHY: More work to do!

MARY: We'll never get through.

BETH: And we always start before dawn every morning, too.

DOROTHY: It wasn't like this before.

MARY: I know.

BETH: Remember when Snow White's mother was alive?

MARY: Yes, she was so good to everyone.

DOROTHY: Not like this queen.

BETH: I'll say. All she ever thinks about is herself.

MARY: And how beautiful she thinks she is.

BETH: I never could understand why the king married that woman.

DOROTHY: I'll bet he thought she'd be a mother for Snow White.

BETH: Well, he couldn't have been more wrong!

MARY: Now he's gone and that wicked queen is all she has.

BETH: Poor Snow White.

MARY: It's so sad.

DOROTHY: Yes, it is . . . Oh, look. Here's Snow White now.

BETH: Just coming to talk to us.

SNOW WHITE: Good morning, everybody. See the flowers I picked in the garden?

MARY: How pretty!

BETH: They're lovely.

SNOW WHITE: I picked them especially for the queen's dressing table.

DOROTHY: That was kind of you.

SNOW WHITE: I thought it might cheer her up and make her be nicer to us.

MARY: Now maybe it will.

BETH: I hope so.

QUEEN: Snow White!

SNOW WHITE: Yes, Ma'am.

QUEEN: What are you doing in my room?

SNOW WHITE: I came to bring you these flowers.

QUEEN: Ah, and just where did you get them?

SNOW WHITE: Out of the garden.

QUEEN: Out of MY garden?

SNOW WHITE: Yes . . . They were so pretty I thought you would like to have some in your room.

QUEEN: Did you now?

SNOW WHITE: Yes, I hope you like them.

QUEEN: How dare you? You had no right to pick those flowers.

SNOW WHITE: But I was just trying to be nice.

QUEEN: You did NOT have my permission.

SNOW WHITE: I'm sorry.

QUEEN: Sorry! That's not enough. You must be punished!

SNOW WHITE: But why?

QUEEN: Leave this minute. I don't want to hear anything you have to say. I must think about your punishment.

SNOW WHITE: (*Bowing her head briefly*) Yes, Ma'am.

QUEEN: Go, all of you, and take these tacky flowers out of my sight.

DOROTHY: As you wish, Ma'am.

(*The others exit.*)

QUEEN: Stupid, ugly people. (*She goes to the mirror and looks at herself.*) How nice it is to see my soft, lovely skin and gorgeous hair . . . and these beautiful hands. (*She holds them up admiring them.*) Yes, such a joy . . . Mirror, Mirror on the wall. Who's the fairest of us all?

(*Lights flash and music starts to play. The sprite of the mirror steps out from it and dances around the room. When the music ends she goes to the queen saying:*)

MIRROR: Oh, Queen, yours is a beauty rare, but Snow White is a thousand times more fair!

QUEEN: Snow White! That child?

(*The mirror nods her head, "yes."*)

QUEEN: Why you must be teasing me.

(*The mirror shakes her head, "no."*)

QUEEN: But I'm much more beautiful.

MIRROR: Oh, no, you're not. Not anymore.

QUEEN: That's untrue.

MIRROR: I never lie. Snow White's much prettier to the eye!

QUEEN: Get out of my sight!

MIRROR: I certainly will, Queen, but I know I'm right!

(*Lights flash again. The music plays and the sprite exits.*)

QUEEN: Snow White! Snow White more beautiful than I! (*She walks around the room thinking.*) Well, I'll fix that. (*She goes to the door and yells:*) Herman, HERMAN: Come here this instant!

HERMAN: (*Enters and bows*) You called, Your Majesty?

QUEEN: Yes, of course.

QUEEN: Herman, do you remember telling me about the huntsman who brought us that delicious pheasant?

HERMAN: Certainly, Your Highness.

QUEEN: Do you know how to get in touch with him?

HERMAN: Why yes, Your Majesty, he just brought us some venison and he's sitting in the kitchen right now.

QUEEN: Excellent. Bring him to me at once.

HERMAN: Very good, Your Highness. (*He exits.*)

QUEEN: Now I will straighten everything out.

(*The huntsman enters and bows.*)

HUNTSMAN: You wanted me, Your Majesty?

QUEEN: Yes. I want to send you on the most important mission of your life.

HUNTSMAN: Very well, Your Highness, whatever you desire.

QUEEN: You are to take my stepdaughter, Snow White, deep into the forest and kill her.

HUNTSMAN: Kill her?

QUEEN: Yes. (*She crosses the room and picks up a jewelry box.*) Then I want you to bring me her heart in this jewelry box.

HUNTSMAN: You must be joking.

QUEEN: I never joke. Do you understand?

HUNTSMAN: Yes, Your Majesty, but I saw that beautiful child in the garden when I came this morning. I don't think I can do that to her.

QUEEN: Of course you can, my man, and if you don't do it YOUR heart will be in the box.

HUNTSMAN: Oh, no!

QUEEN: Oh, yes . . . or . . . you can be handsomely rewarded. It's your choice.

HUNTSMAN: (*He pauses, thinking, shakes his head sadly, then:*) All right. I suppose I have to do it.

QUEEN: Yes.

HUNTSMAN: When do you want me to leave?

QUEEN: Now. And remember if you do not follow my instructions you will pay with your life!

HUNTSMAN: I understand.

QUEEN: Good. Now be gone. Just remember I MUST be obeyed!

(*The huntsman bows to the queen and leaves.*)

QUEEN: (*Smiling to herself*) Soon we shall see who is the fairest in the land.

CURTAIN

SCENE II. The forest.

SNOW WHITE: I love it here in the woods.

HUNTSMAN: It is nice.

SNOW WHITE: The trees are all so pretty.

HUNTSMAN: I like them, too.

SNOW WHITE: And it's fun to watch the rabbits and squirrels running around.

HUNTSMAN: Yes, I've always liked that.

SNOW WHITE: But you don't seem very happy.

HUNTSMAN: Today is different.

SNOW WHITE: But I thought you liked me. I like you.

HUNTSMAN: Oh, I do like you.

SNOW WHITE: Then?

HUNTSMAN: I like you too much. That's the trouble.

SNOW WHITE: I don't understand.

HUNTSMAN: It's the queen, Snow White.

SNOW WHITE: The queen?

HUNTSMAN: Yes. She wants me to kill you.

SNOW WHITE: Kill me! But why would she want to do that? I'm nice to her.

HUNTSMAN: I believe you.

SNOW WHITE: Then why kill me?

HUNTSMAN: Because I have to.

SNOW WHITE: I don't understand.

HUNTSMAN: She told me to put your heart in this box and take it to her, or she would have me killed.

SNOW WHITE: Did she mean it?

HUNTSMAN: I'm afraid so.

SNOW WHITE: (*Going down on her knees, begging*) Please, please, don't kill me.

HUNTSMAN: I have to.

SNOW WHITE: Please.

HUNTSMAN: I don't want to, but what can I do?

SNOW WHITE: I know. You could kill some animal and put its heart in the box.

HUNTSMAN: That might work . . . Yes, yes, it just might!

SNOW WHITE: Then, please, please, do it. I'll stay in the woods.

HUNTSMAN: And never go back to the palace?

SNOW WHITE: Never.

HUNTSMAN: Do you promise?

SNOW WHITE: I promise.

HUNTSMAN: Then I'll do it.

SNOW WHITE: Thank you. Oh, thank you.

HUNTSMAN: I can't help you anymore.

SNOW WHITE: I understand. I'll manage here some way.

HUNTSMAN: I think you will.

SNOW WHITE: I'm sure I can.

HUNTSMAN: Then goodbye, Snow White. I wish you the best of luck.

SNOW WHITE: Thank you. I shall always remember your kindness.

CURTAIN

SCENE III. The home of the dwarfs.

A suggestion of furniture is all that is necessary—a table with some food on it, and one or two chairs. Lots of clothing is scattered on the floor. A broom should be visible. Snow White's voice can be heard from outside as the scene opens.

SNOW WHITE: Please, please let me in. I'm so frightened out here in the forest. . . . Please let me in. . . . I don't think anyone is at home. I'll just try the door and see if it's open, then I can go in and be safe for a while and rest. (*She opens the door and enters.*) It IS open! What a darling little house. Everything is so tiny. . . . It must be a doll's house, or maybe children live here who have no mother. It certainly is a mess. . . . Maybe if I clean up everything they'll let me stay. (*She goes to work picking up and straightening the room.*). . . . There. That looks better already. . . . Do you suppose they'll mind if I eat this roll that's left over? I'll bet they wouldn't notice that it's gone. . . . If they do I can work to pay for it. . . . I'm so hungry I'm going to do it. . . . (*She eats some of the roll.*) That's better. I'm tired from all that running. I think I'll just lie down here and rest for a while. (*She lies down and immediately falls asleep.*)

(*The dwarfs enter talking.*)

DWARF #1: We sure got a lot done today.

DWARF #2: Yes, but now we have to clean up our dirty old house.

DWARF #3: Let's wait until tomorrow. I'm too tired now.

DWARF #4: I agree. We've worked all day.

DWARF #5: Maybe it won't take too long.

DWARF #6: We shouldn't have to work in the mine and do all the housework, too.

DWARF #2: Right! One job's enough.

DWARF #1: Now fellows . . .

DWARF #7: But . . .

DWARF #2: Oh, be quiet.

DWARF #7: But . . .

DWARF #1: Yes. What do you want?

DWARF #7: We're not going to have to do anything to the house. It's all cleaned up!

DWARF #5: Why, you're right!

(*They all start to look around the room.*)

DWARF #3: Everything IS clean.

DWARF #1: I don't understand.

DWARF #2: I know. Who could have done it?

DWARF #6: I think whoever did it is over there!

(*The dwarfs rush over to Snow White who has her face turned away from them. They stand looking at her, obviously afraid.*)

DWARF #3: I think it's asleep.

DWARF #4: Is it a goblin?

DWARF #7: Maybe it's a ghost.

DWARF #5: (*Moving to look at Snow White's face.*) Well, whatever it is, it's mighty pretty.

(*Snow White awakens, stretches, and gets up.*)

DWARF #1: Why bless my soul. It's a girl!

SNOW WHITE: And you're not children. I thought you were.

DWARF #7: No, we're dwarfs.

DWARF #2: What are you doing here in our house?

SNOW WHITE: I was so afraid out in the woods. I called and

nobody answered, and since the door was open I came in. I hope you don't mind. I didn't hurt anything.

DWARF #5: We can see that.

DWARF #3: You even cleaned up for us.

SNOW WHITE: I thought it might be a nice surprise.

DWARF #2: Oh, it was.

DWARF #6: Yes, we really liked that.

DWARF #1 But who are you and what are you doing here?

DWARF #7: Are you lost?

DWARF #1: She must be, and I bet your parents are worried sick about you.

SNOW WHITE: No. My parents are dead. I have no one except my stepmother and she hates me. She hates me so much she sent me into the woods so she could have me killed.

OTHERS: No.

SNOW WHITE: Yes, that's why I'm here.

DWARF #1: You poor child. You must have been terribly afraid.

SNOW WHITE: I was. The woods are beautiful but they can be frightening when it starts getting dark.

DWARF #7: I know.

SNOW WHITE: Why do you live way out here by yourselves?

DWARF #5: It's just easier that way.

SNOW WHITE: What do you mean?

DWARF #3: He means that out here people don't look at us funny because we're little.

DWARF #4: Or point at us and laugh.

DWARF #6: Or ask us questions.

SNOW WHITE: You poor things.

DWARF #7: Way out here by ourselves we can just forget we're different.

DWARF #2: But sometimes it does get a little lonely.

SNOW WHITE: You need a friend.

DWARF #5: That would be nice.

SNOW WHITE: Let me stay with you and I'll be your friend.

DWARF #1: Well, I don't know.

SNOW WHITE: And I'll be here to talk to you, and listen to what you have to say.

DWARF #3: That would be nice.

SNOW WHITE: And I'll be here waiting for you every day when you come back.

DWARF #5: And I bet you'd help clean up, like you did today.

SNOW WHITE: Of course I would. And I can cook, and iron, and wash, and sew, too. Maybe not real well, but I can learn.

DWARF #7: That sounds like a good idea to me.

DWARF #2: I don't know. It would probably cause problems.

DWARF #1: I think this requires a conference, don't you? (*The others nod their heads "yes," so he leads them to a corner of the room and they huddle together. They talk briefly, then pull apart, look at Snow White and shake their heads "no," and go back into the huddle. They talk briefly and again shake their heads "no." Snow White watches anxiously. The dwarfs continue talking, and this time nod their heads "yes." Dwarf #1 leaves the others and walks over to Snow White.*)

DWARF #1: We've decided, Miss, ah . . .

SNOW WHITE: My name is Snow White. Will you let me stay?

DWARF #7: We all voted YES.

SNOW WHITE: That's wonderful. I promise I'll make you glad you did.

DWARF #2: You'd better.

SNOW WHITE: Oh, I will.

DWARF #6: (*Coming up to her shyly*) I'm glad you're going to stay with us.

SNOW WHITE: Thank you. So am I. We're all going to be great friends.

CURTAIN

SCENE IV. The Palace.
   The Queen is alone talking to herself.

QUEEN: At last Snow White is gone. I'm finally rid of her! The huntsman DID obey me. I was afraid for a while that she might charm him into letting her go. . . . I'm sure she tried. But no, he wouldn't have paid attention to her after seeing me. He must have been overwhelmed by my beauty. . . . That's it. I saw him admiring my gorgeous hair and lovely skin and sparkling eyes. . . . No man can resist me. (*She walks to the mirror.*) Now, magic mirror on the wall, who is the fairest one of all?

(*Lights flash and the mirror sprite steps into the room.*)

MIRROR: Oh, Queen, yours is a beauty rare, but Snow White's a thousand times more fair.

QUEEN: Snow White? But she is dead.

MIRROR: With seven dwarfs she's living now. The loveliest lady still, I vow.

QUEEN: She's alive! Oh-h-h-h! She's still alive! He tricked me! He lied!. . . . I shall just have to do away with her myself. . . . Yes, I can do that. . . . What a pleasure it will be!. . . . Serves her right. (*The Queen is walking around the room thinking out loud.*) Now I have a plan. I know just how to fix her so she will bother me no more. How wonderful my life will be, when from Snow White I'm finally free!

CURTAIN

SCENE V. Outside the dwarfs' house.

DWARF #7: Gee, it's nice to have a girl like you here, Snow White.

DWARF #6: He means it's nice to have YOU here.

SNOW WHITE: I'm so happy you decided to let me stay.

DWARF #5: We're all glad, too.

SNOW WHITE: I love it here with you.

DWARF #7: It's nice for us to have someone to talk to.

DWARF #4: And play games with.

DWARF #3: And we don't have to work all the time either.

SNOW WHITE: That's just what I wanted.

DWARF #6: I like having time to play my guitar more.

DWARF #2: But you do it too much. You're always bothering us.

SNOW WHITE: Not me. I like to hear you play and it's fun to dance to the music.

(*This is a good time to have Snow White and the dwarfs do a little dance. It is not necessary, but does add to the play. Any dance or music will do.*)

DWARF #1: We all love you, Snow White. Don't we, fellows? (*They all nod.*) Now you go right on in the house as soon as we leave.

DWARF #5: And don't forget to lock the door.

SNOW WHITE: All right.

DWARF #6: Don't let anyone in, either.

SNOW WHITE: No, I won't.

DWARF #1: Promise?

SNOW WHITE: Of course I promise. Now you fellows quit worrying about me. OK? (*They nod yes.*) Good, then you'd better get going to work.

DWARF #7: Do I have to go? I could stay and keep Snow White company.

DWARF #2: You could, but that would leave us with all your work to do.

DWARF #7: That's not what I meant.

DWARF #5: Of course, it wasn't.

DWARF #1: But you just come along with us.

DWARF #7: All right.

OTHERS: Good-bye.

SNOW WHITE: I'll have a good dinner ready when you get back.

DWARFS: Fine. Good-bye.

(*Snow White waves to the dwarfs as they exit. Her back is to the queen who enters disguised as an old woman. She is carrying a basket of apples.*)

QUEEN: Would you like a nice apple, dearie?

SNOW WHITE: Oh, you startled me.

QUEEN: Why I didn't mean to. I thought you might like to have this lovely, rosy apple. They're getting too heavy to carry.

SNOW WHITE: Thank you. It looks delicious.

QUEEN: Oh, it is. Here. Go on and eat it. I'll bet you're hungry.

SNOW WHITE: I am, a little bit.

QUEEN: Then go ahead and get started. If you want more you can have them.

SNOW WHITE: You're very kind, but I can't take your apples.

QUEEN: Of course, you can.

SNOW WHITE: No, I really can't. I'm not allowed to.

QUEEN: What's the matter? Are you afraid of being poisoned?

SNOW WHITE: Well, yes.

QUEEN: Oh, you poor dear. Now I understand.

SNOW WHITE: You do?

QUEEN: Yes, but I'll help you. Look. I'll take a bite myself just so you'll know that my apple's all right.

SNOW WHITE: If you like.

QUEEN: (*Takes a bite out of the apple and hands it to Snow White.*) Hmmm. This is delicious. Best one I've eaten. You take it. Enjoy the rest. (*Spitting the bite into a handkerchief*)

SNOW WHITE: It seems like it's all right.

QUEEN: I just showed you it was. You don't have a thing to worry about.

SNOW WHITE: It does look good.

QUEEN: It is. Go on. Eat it.

SNOW WHITE: But I promised.

QUEEN: No one will ever know. See, I'm just fine, and I want you to have a little treat.

SNOW WHITE: All right, then I will have some. Thank you.

QUEEN: Fine. You can have all you want.

(*Snow White takes a bite and then falls to the ground.*)

QUEEN: White as snow. Red as blood. You'll soon be as ugly as a puddle of mud. Your dwarfs can't save you from the work of my hand. I'll soon be the fairest in all the land. (*She gives a loud, evil laugh.*) Ha! Ha! (*She exits.*)

CURTAIN

SCENE VI. Several hours later.
   Snow White is still lying on the ground. The dwarfs enter.

DWARF #1: I wonder what Snow White has fixed for supper.

DWARF #5: I don't know, but I'll bet it's good.

DWARF #7: Like always.

DWARF #3: I hope it's ready. I'm hungry.

DWARF #4: Look! There on the ground.

DWARF #1: It's Snow White!

DWARF #5: Snow White?

(*They hurry to her side.*)

DWARF #7: What's the matter with her?

DWARF #6: Is she sick?

DWARF #3 Maybe she's asleep.

DWARF #1: I think . . . she's . . . dead.

DWARF #2: Oh, no.

DWARF #5: Not our beautiful Snow White.

DWARF #7: I should have stayed with her.

DWARF #2: And we should have let you.

(*The dwarfs huddle around Snow White crying softly. There is a long pause before the page enters.*)

PAGE: Excuse me.

DWARF #1: Yes?

PAGE: I don't want to interrupt, but I have a problem.

DWARF #1: How can I help you?

PAGE: I'm a page traveling with Queen Rebecca and her son, Prince Ivan.

DWARF #5: We've heard of them.

PAGE: Yes. We're from the country just south of here and are on our way home.

DWARF #3: Yes?

PAGE: But we are lost.

DWARF #7: That's too bad.

PAGE: Can you tell me the way to our palace?

DWARF #1: That's easy. It's not far from here.

DWARF #4: You're on the right road.

DWARF #1: Tell the others to come on through here.

PAGE: Thank you. I'll go get them. (*He exits.*)

(*The dwarfs turn back toward Snow White and cry into their handkerchiefs. Prince Ivan and Queen Rebecca enter, followed by Merritt.*)

PRINCE: Mother, I know you must be tired.

REBECCA: Yes, but I feel more rested just knowing we're not lost.

PRINCE: We were going the right way all the time.

REBECCA: Yes, dear.

PRINCE: Why don't you go over there and sit in the shade of the tree while I talk to the men who gave us directions.

REBECCA: Of course. Take all the time you need.

PRINCE: You'll be all right?

REBECCA: Certainly. I have Merritt and she always takes good care of me.

MERRITT: Thank you, Your Majesty.

PRINCE: (*To the page*) Igor, you stay with mother while I'm talking to those men. (*He points toward the dwarfs.*)

PAGE: Certainly, Sir.

REBECCA: Go on, dear. Don't worry. We'll be just fine.

(*Rebecca, Merritt, and Igor all sit on the ground, and the Prince crosses to the dwarfs.*)

PRINCE: You seem so sad. Can I help you?

DWARF #1: No. Nothing can be done for her now.

PRINCE: I'm so sorry.

DWARF #7: We are, too.

DWARF #5: Yes, she was our best friend in the world.

PRINCE: Was?

DWARF #2: Yes. We can't get her to move or talk.

DWARF #7: Or anything.

PRINCE: No wonder you are so sad.

DWARF #3: It breaks my heart.

PRINCE: Let me see her. . . . Why she's beautiful.

DWARF #3: Yes, she's our lovely little Snow White.

PRINCE: Snow White. That's the name of the princess of your country.

DWARF #1: We know. That's her.

PRINCE: Her? We've just come from her palace where we went to see her, but the queen said she'd died very suddenly a few weeks ago.

DWARF #3: No. It was only today.

PRINCE: That's strange. Let me get closer. Maybe I can awaken her.

DWARF #1: Go ahead.

PRINCE: Snow White . . . Snow White. (*He touches her forehead and her wrist for a pulse.*) Let's sit her up. Maybe that will help. (*A dwarf holds her up.*) Snow White, wake up. (*He shakes her gently.*)

DWARF #1: Why she just spat out a bite of an apple.

DWARF #2: She must have been poisoned with that.

PRINCE: Snow White. Wake up.

SNOW WHITE: (*Moving forward*) Where am I?

(*The dwarfs look at her, then move to her side, join hands, and start to dance in a circle.*)

DWARF #5: She's moving!

DWARF #3: She's not dead.

DWARF #6: She can talk.

DWARF #2: We have our Snow White back again.

SNOW WHITE: Who are you?

PRINCE: I'm Prince Ivan from the country just south of here.

SNOW WHITE: Prince Ivan?

PRINCE: And that is my mother, Queen Rebecca.

DWARF #1: They've been to your palace looking for you, but your stepmother told them you were dead.

PRINCE: Yes. That's what she said. You see, I'd heard so much about you I had decided I had to have you as my bride. We had gone to see if you would have me.

SNOW WHITE: But what happened to the old woman with the apples?

DWARF #4: What old woman?

SNOW WHITE: The one who gave me the apple.

DWARF #1: It must have been your stepmother in disguise.

SNOW WHITE: I thought that something about her seemed familiar. Now that I think about it, their voices were alike.

DWARF #6: Then it was she!

DWARF #5: To think she came here to kill you.

SNOW WHITE: That's frightening.

PRINCE: If you'll come with my mother and me to our country you won't ever have to be afraid of your stepmother again. Will you come with us?

SNOW WHITE: You're sure you want me to come?

PRINCE: That's why we came. To get you.

SNOW WHITE: And you'll see that I'm safe?

PRINCE: With my life. I want you to be my wife.

SNOW WHITE: But what about my friends here? Can they come to visit us?

PRINCE: Of course. Any time they want.

SNOW WHITE: (*To the dwarfs*) Will you come?

DWARF #1: No one could keep us away.

DWARF #7: We love you, Snow White.

DWARF #6: Yes, we do.

DWARF #5: We worry about you here with us. There you'd be safe.

SNOW WHITE: You want me to go, too?

DWARF #1: We do, because we care about you.

PRINCE: (*To Snow White*) Then you'll do it? You'll come with me?

SNOW WHITE: All right then, I will.

PRINCE: And you'll be my wife?

SNOW WHITE: . . . And be your wife.

PRINCE: And I'll see that you live happily . . . all your life!

CURTAIN

THE TWO BAD BARGAINS

Cast of Characters

Vladimir, a caring man
Alec, his friend
Vladimir's father
Frederick, a sailor
Slave #1
Slave #2
Slave #3
Slave #4
Sergeant, guards prisoners
Old man, a prisoner
Prisoner #2
Prisoner #3
Soldier, helps the sergeant
Harold, chief minister
King, Helene's father
1st guard
2nd guard

Deborah, Vladimir's sister
Laura, Vladimir's sister
Pamela, Vladimir's sister
Vladimir's mother
Helene, a princess
Rachel, her nurse
Queen, Helene's mother
Lady-in-waiting
Maid, the queen's servant

Production Notes

A play written for seventeen boys and nine girls. Additional slaves and prisoners may be added as needed. Girls may play the parts of slaves and prisoners if more girls' parts are required. The lady-in-waiting and maid may be played by one person. The roles of the slaves and prisoners may be combined if you want fewer people.

Discussion Questions

Use the following for discussion or as topics for creative writing.

1. Vladimir and his sisters seem to have a good relationship. This is not true of all brothers and sisters. Often there is resentment between them. What reasons can you give for this?
2. Why do you think Vladimir and his sisters were so close? What can family members do to have better relationships?
3. Is it all right to be angry with someone in your family? How can you show it? What should you do if you are hurt and angry with someone?
4. Was Vladimir's father justified in being angry with him? Why, or why not?
5. Do you think it was acceptable for Vladimir to give away his cargo to save people he did not know?
6. Vladimir cared about animals as well as people. Do we have an obligation to take care of our pets? What do pets need? What do they give us in return? Do animals have feelings? Write a story about a child who has a very special pet.
7. The old man returned Vladimir's kindness by taking care of him. Should we expect others to be nice to us if we are good to them? Is it a good idea to be kind to people expecting them to return our consideration?

8. Vladimir's father was very angry with him for a time. Can we control our emotions? Do you think that people sometimes make themselves happy or discontented. What can we do to make ourselves feel better?

9. The king was good to Harold, yet Harold treated him and his family badly. Why are people sometimes unkind to the ones who love them the most and treat them the best? What can we do if this happens to us?

10. Vladimir felt it was wrong to own slaves. How do you think you would feel if you were a slave? Write a paragraph describing your feelings.

11. Imagine that you and your family are slaves. Write a story that tells what happens when you are sold and sent away to live by yourself.

12. Write a story about a boy or girl who is angry and unhappy. Have a happy ending to the story because of something the boy or girl did to make the situation better.

Enrichment Activities

Suggestions for the teacher. For research purposes set the play in Greece in the first half of the nineteenth century. Assign or have students select an activity from each category and teach the others in the class what they have learned. Require the students to write one or two questions to be asked at the completion of their reports. Students may do the assignments individually or as teams.

Do one of the following projects:

1. Make a model of an ancient Greek theater.
2. Make a relief map of Greece.
3. Make a map of Greece during the fourth century B.C. and a map of Greece today.
4. Dress a doll to show the clothing worn in ancient Greece.
5. Dress a doll to show the national costume of Greece.
6. Make illustrations of the clothing worn in ancient Greece.

7. Make illustrations of the clothing worn in Greece in the 19th century.
8. Make a model of the Parthenon.
9. Make a poster showing the Greek alphabet with a translation to English.

Write a report on one of the following topics:

1. The first Olympic games.
2. Greek mythology.
3. Alexander the Great
4. The Trojan Horse
5. Greece. Tell about the people, customs, climate, manufacturing, and food.
6. The education of children in ancient Greece
7. Aesop was a Greek slave who lived more than 2,500 years ago. He wrote many fables. Write about one of Aesop's fables in your own words. Give the moral of the story. Some suggestions are as follows:

"The Fox and the Grapes"
"The Tortoise and the Hare"
"The Fox and the Goat"
"The Farmer and the Fox"
"The North Wind and the Sun"
"The Boy Who Cried Wolf"
"The Dog and His Reflection"
"The Ant and the Grasshopper"
"The Goose That Laid the Golden Egg"
"The House Mouse and the Field Mouse"

8. The ancient Greeks used mythology to explain happenings they could not understand. Tell the story of one of the following in your own words: Zeus, Apollo, Ares, Poseidon, Hermes, Eros, Hera, Dionysus, Demeter, Ceres, Atalanta, Proserpina, and the Unicorn.

The Two Bad Bargains—Play Script

SCENE I. The deck of Vladimir's ship.

Vladimir is talking to his three sisters who have come to tell him good-bye before he sails.

DEBORAH: Vladimir, it's a beautiful ship. I wish I were going with you.

PAMELA: Yes, just think, if we had been boys instead of girls we'd be getting ships like this and be off on a big adventure.

VLADIMIR: I wish I could take you with me, if that's what you really want.

LAURA: And you'd do it, too. We know you would.

DEBORAH: That's what worries us, your going off by yourself.

LAURA: You're so soft-hearted we're afraid you'll stop to give every fish in the ocean a ride.

PAMELA: So they won't have to swim so far.

VLADIMIR: Now, even I know better than that!

LAURA: But we remember all the lost dogs you've brought home to be fed and cared for.

DEBORAH: And the birds with the broken wings.

PAMELA: To say nothing of the fox with the hurt paw.

VLADIMIR: But they all needed help!

LAURA: And you were the one who gave it to them.

VLADIMIR: Somebody had to, or they would have died.

LAURA: We know, little brother, you're a softy, but that's what we like best about you, isn't it?

PAMELA: That, and because you're always so kind to us.

VLADIMIR: It's easy with you three.

DEBORAH: Not all the time.

VLADIMIR: Enough of it.

LAURA: Well, we're all going to worry about you out there without us.

PAMELA: Thank goodness he'll have Alec to keep him in line.

DEBORAH: Be sure you listen to him, too.

PAMELA: He's very level-headed.

VLADIMIR: And I'm not?

LAURA: We just don't want anyone to take advantage of you.

DEBORAH: Because you're so nice.

VLADIMIR: All right. I'll watch out.

DEBORAH: Be sure to, brother dear, we're depending on it.

(*Vladimir's mother and father and Alec enter.*)

FATHER: Well, son, it looks like everything is all ready to go.

MOTHER: Yes, Alec has just given us the nicest tour of the ship.

ALEC: My pleasure.

LAURA: We just wish we were going, too.

FATHER: Now girls, you know better than that.

MOTHER: You're sure there's enough food on board to last all those days you're planning to be at sea?

FATHER: Certainly there is. The chief cook's gone over everything at least three times.

MOTHER: Well, I'm still concerned.

LAURA: We know, mother, we're going to worry about him, too.

VLADIMIR: Everything's going to be just fine. You'll see.

FATHER: Of course it will.

ALEC: He'll have me if he has any questions.

VLADIMIR: Questions!

FATHER: I was glad to see for myself that you're loaded with enough cargo so that when you get out in the trading world you'll be able to make yourself a rich man.

VLADIMIR: I know, Father, and I thank you.

FATHER: I'm sure you do, Vladimir. It's because you've always been such an appreciative son that we're doing this for you.

PAMELA: Yes, now you're going to be a rich one, too, all on your own.

LAURA: Just don't forget to bring us some pretty silks.

DEBORAH: And perfumes.

MOTHER: And stay safe. Don't take any chances you don't have to.

VLADIMIR: All right, mother.

FATHER: Have a successful trip.

VLADIMIR: I'll try, sir.

FATHER: Then we'd better tell you good-bye.

DEBORAH: Good-bye, Vladimir.

VLADIMIR: Thank you for coming to see us off.

PAMELA: Good-bye, brother.

VLADIMIR: Good-bye.

OTHERS: Good-bye.

CURTAIN

SCENE II. The deck of Vladimir's ship.
It is four weeks later. The ship is docked at a Turkish port. Vladimir and Alec are on deck. The sounds of people moaning and weeping can be heard off stage.

VLADIMIR: Those poor people on the boat docked next to ours sound so miserable.

ALEC: They really do.

VLADIMIR: I can't stand to hear them crying. Maybe we can help them.

ALEC: I knew you were going to say that.

VLADIMIR: We have to see if we can. I'm going to try to talk to their captain. (*Calling offstage*) Frederick.

FREDERICK: Aye, aye, sir. (*Entering*)

VLADIMIR: Go talk to the sailors on the next boat. Tell them I would like to meet with their captain. Ask if he will come up on deck for a few minutes.

FREDERICK: As you wish, sir. (*He exits.*)

ALEC: I don't like this situation, Vladimir.

VLADIMIR: And I don't like their cries for help.

ALEC: I know. Just be careful.

FREDERICK: (*Entering*) I talked to the sailors, sir. They say that their captain will be up in a few moments.

VLADIMIR: Very good, Frederick.

(*Frederick exits. There is a voice from offstage.*)

CAPTAIN: You wanted to talk to me?

VLADIMIR: Yes, we're concerned. Why is there so much crying and wailing coming from your hold?

CAPTAIN: We have captured a shipload of slaves to sell in the great slave market at Istanbul. It is those who are chained who are weeping.

VLADIMIR: How much are they worth . . . your shipload of slaves?

CAPTAIN: As much as all the cargo you're carrying on your ship.

ALEC: I know what you're thinking, but remember your father. What would he say?

VLADIMIR: He would probably be very angry.

ALEC: Can you blame him?

VLADIMIR: No, but it isn't right for people to make others their slaves.

ALEC: Yet you can't stop them.

VLADIMIR: But I can stop this one boat from doing it, and that will be some help.

ALEC: I don't know . . .

VLADIMIR: I do know. I'm going to buy those poor slaves and set them free.

ALEC: Vladimir . . .

VLADIMIR: My mind's made up. Captain?

CAPTAIN: Yes.

VLADIMIR: You may have the cargo. I've decided to buy your slaves.

ALEC: You should have seen if he would take less for them.

CAPTAIN: Very good. I'll have my crew get them over to your ship so they can start moving things over to my vessel. We need to get back to our home port right away.

VLADIMIR: Fine. (*Calling offstage*) Frederick.

FREDERICK: (*Entering*) You wanted me, sir?

VLADIMIR: As soon as the slaves are put on board send them to me.

FREDERICK: Aye, aye, sir. (*He exits.*)

ALEC: I hope you know what you're doing.

VLADIMIR: I know I'm doing the right thing for those poor people.

FREDERICK: They're here now, sir. (*Entering*)

VLADIMIR: Good. Bring them to me.

(*A group of slaves who are chained together enter. They are ragged and dirty, and seem very much afraid.*)

VLADIMIR: Don't be frightened. I am your friend.

SLAVE #1: Our friend?

VLADIMIR: Yes. I only bought you to set you free.

SLAVE #2: Do you mean that?

SLAVE #3: This is not a cruel joke?

VLADIMIR: It is no joke at all. What I said was true.

SLAVE #4: We will not be slaves anymore?

VLADIMIR: That is correct. As soon as we can get the chains off you may do as you like. Go ashore or stay with the ship until we get to your home ports.

SLAVE #1: Kind sir, (*He and the others fall on their knees.*) how can we thank you?

VLADIMIR: Knowing your cries have stopped will be my payment.

SLAVE #2: But that is so little.

VLADIMIR: It is enough. Men should not be slaves of others. Go now. My men will get the chains off and give you something to eat.

SLAVE #3: Thank you, master.

VLADIMIR: I am not your master. You are free.

SLAVE #4: You're a good man.

SLAVE #1: We'll never forget you.

SLAVE #2: You'll always be in our prayers.

SLAVE #3: Thank you.

(*They leave. An old woman and a young girl stay behind.*)

RACHEL: Sir, I am Rachel. I am a nurse, and this is my ward, Helene.

VLADIMIR: Welcome.

RACHEL: We want to ask if we can stay with you on your ship.

VLADIMIR: But I don't understand. You are free to leave.

RACHEL: Our home is so far away. We don't know how to get there.

HELENE: Yes, my father is the king of a large country. One day we were outside the palace and we were taken prisoner.

RACHEL: We've been slaves for months. We don't know how to get back home.

VLADIMIR: Now I understand. Maybe we can help you find your way.

HELENE: Would you, sir?

VLADIMIR: Of course we will.

RACHEL: And we can stay with you until you do?

VLADIMIR: Until we do. Don't be afraid anymore. I will take care of you both.

HELENE: You are such a good man.

ALEC: Yes, but a foolish one, I'm afraid.

VLADIMIR: That may be, Alec. But I know I did what was right. Everything will work out fine.

CURTAIN

SCENE III. The home of Vladimir's parents.

Vladimir and Helene have just entered. His mother and sisters hurry to the door to greet them.

MOTHER: Vladimir, how good it is to have you here.

LAURA: And you, too, Helene. (*She gives her a hug.*)

PAMELA: Yes, now that you're Vladimir's wife we have a new sister.

DEBORAH: And we're glad that it's you.

MOTHER: Yes, welcome to our home.

HELENE: Thank you. You're very kind.

VLADIMIR: It's good to be here with you.

MOTHER: We've all missed you and wanted to see you.

PAMELA: Father wouldn't let us have you come to see us.

VLADIMIR: I know. I understand.

DEBORAH: He was so furious.

LAURA: He'd just say over and over, "How could he have been so foolish? I sent him away with a valuable cargo and all he brought back were two empty mouths to feed."

PAMELA: You don't know how hard it was to convince him that he should forgive and forget.

MOTHER: Your father can be very difficult at times.

HELENE: If he could have seen how miserable all of the slaves were on that ship, I think he would have understood.

LAURA: Is it true that you were all chained to each other?

HELENE: Yes, and the chains hurt. We could hardly move.

VLADIMIR: No wonder they were crying and wailing.

HELENE: And we didn't know where we were going.

VLADIMIR: Or who was going to buy them.

HELENE: Or what they would make us do.

MOTHER: You poor dear. I'm glad Vladimir got you away.

LAURA: We are, too.

PAMELA: Yes, and now you don't have to be afraid any more.

DEBORAH: Not even when Vladimir's gone. You'll be here with us.

(*Father enters.*)

FATHER: I understand that the ship is all laden and ready to leave.

VLADIMIR: Yes, Father. We leave in the morning.

FATHER: You know I expect you to use good judgment with your cargo this time, son.

MOTHER: But he wouldn't be our Vladimir if he didn't care about what happens to other people.

FATHER: That's true. But he should also care about what happens to his poor old father and mother if he gives away all of our money.

LAURA: Which I'm sure our brother won't do.

PAMELA: Even kindhearted Vladimir's bound to have learned his lesson.

DEBORAH: And I've learned that it's time to eat.

MOTHER: Come. We must all go celebrate having our family together again.

PAMELA: And our having a new sister called Helene!

CURTAIN

SCENE V. A street in a port city.
   It is three weeks later. Vladimir and Alec are walking down the street of a strange city.

ALEC: It really seems good to be on land again.

VLADIMIR: Yes, I was getting tired of rocking up and down on that old ship, too.

ALEC: I know the crew's happy to be off for awhile.

VLADIMIR: This will give us time to look for the best deals we can make with our cargo.

ALEC: Your father would be happy to hear you talking like that.

VLADIMIR: I know.

(*A group of ragged prisoners corralled by several soldiers enter.*)

SERGEANT: Hurry it up. Stop dawdling. This walk is taking twice as long as it should.

OLD MAN: But I'm so thirsty. Water. Won't you give me water?

SERGEANT: Water? We hardly have enough for ourselves.

VLADIMIR: Here. May I give him some of mine?

SERGEANT: Well, I guess so, if you're foolish enough to do it.

VLADIMIR: Can't you see he's a tired old man?

SOLDIER: So?

VLADIMIR: And the others don't look much better. How long has it been since they've had anything to eat or drink?

SERGEANT: This morning.

ALEC: They've been walking in the hot sun with nothing since then?

SERGEANT: They'll have plenty of time to rest up and cool down where they're going.

VLADIMIR: Where are you taking these poor prisoners?

SOLDIER: To the dungeons.

VLADIMIR: Why? What have they done?

SERGEANT: They cannot pay the king's taxes.

ALEC: And for that they go to prison?

SOLDIER: It's the law.

VLADIMIR: How long will they be there?

SERGEANT: Until they can pay.

SOLDIER: And they won't be able to pay as long as they're rotting in the dungeon.

VLADIMIR: That's terrible.

OLD MAN: Please help us.

PRISONER #2: Please.

PRISONER #3: You're our only chance.

VLADIMIR: I wish I could help you.

ALEC: We both do, but he can't.

SERGEANT: Come on now. We've already wasted too much time.

OLD MAN: Please.

(*Vladimir turns and starts to walk away. He pauses and turns back to the sergeant.*)

VLADIMIR: Who would I go to talk to about having these prisoners released?

SERGEANT: The chief magistrate of the city.

ALEC: Vladimir. Remember your father.

VLADIMIR: Is his office far from here?

SOLDIER: No, only about a five-minute walk.

VLADIMIR: I want to talk with him.

SERGEANT: About what?

VLADIMIR: Seeing how much it would cost to get these people freed.

ALEC: But, Vladimir.

VLADIMIR: Will you wait for me? Just a little while?

SOLDIER: Maybe we could be talked into it.

VLADIMIR: For a fee, or course.

SERGEANT: Well, I guess we could rest a bit.

VLADIMIR: Good. See this gold chain. It's yours if you are still here when we return.

SERGEANT: You're sure it's gold?

VLADIMIR: My father would have given me nothing else.

SERGEANT: Then I guess we can stay, if you hurry.

VLADIMIR: We will. It shouldn't take long to make a deal.

ALEC: Do you know what you're doing?

VLADIMIR: I know. I couldn't let them go to the dungeons to die when I could keep them from it.

ALEC: Oh, Vladimir. You're a good man. But what will ever become of you?

CURTAIN

SCENE V. On the ship.

Two years later in a port city far from Vladimir's home. He and Alec are aboard Vladimir's ship. There are a desk and chair and rug on stage.

ALEC: I've got to admit I was wrong, Vladimir.

VLADIMIR: How's that, Alec?

ALEC: I didn't think you and I would ever be together again in a strange country with your boat docked at the port.

VLADIMIR: I didn't either, Alec. My father's really a very kind and forgiving man.

ALEC: Even though it did take him two years!

VLADIMIR: But I couldn't blame him.

ALEC: I couldn't either.

VLADIMIR: Still there was just no way I could have left those prisoners to die in that dungeon when they had done nothing wrong.

ALEC: But to give all your cargo for them?

VLADIMIR: The chief magistrate wouldn't take less.

ALEC: But now you've learned your lesson?

VLADIMIR: I'm going to stay away from all prisoners and slaves.

ALEC: And don't forget you promised your sisters to stay away from all stray birds and dogs and cats.

VLADIMIR: And foxes with hurt paws! See? I remember.

ALEC: Just don't forget! (*Frederick enters.*)

FREDERICK: Sir, there's a man who says he's a representative of the king who requests permission to come aboard.

VLADIMIR: That's strange.

ALEC: I agree.

VLADIMIR: Tell him he may board, then bring him to me.

FREDERICK: Very good, sir. (*He exits.*)

VLADIMIR: I wonder what this is all about?

ALEC: I wouldn't know.

(*Frederick re-enters with a well-dressed man. Alec and Vladimir rise to greet him.*)

VLADIMIR: Good day, sir. You're welcome aboard my ship.

HAROLD: Thank you. I am Harold, Chief Minister to his royal highness, King Adolph.

VLADIMIR: And what may I do to be of service to his majesty?

HAROLD: He and Queen Eugenia were out for a ride in their carriage and saw your ship. They are outside now and would like to request your permission to enter and talk to you.

VLADIMIR: Of course. It will be my pleasure. Tell them to come on board immediately.

HAROLD: Very well. (*He exits.*)

VLADIMIR: Quick, Frederick and Alec. Help me straighten up.

(*The three hurry about the room getting it in order. Frederick sweeps some dirt under a small rug. He has just finished when King Adolph, Queen Eugenia, Harold, and the queen's lady-in-waiting enter. Vladimir, Alec, and Frederick bow.*)

KING: Thank you for letting us come aboard.

VLADIMIR: It is an honor for us, Your Highness.

KING: We've come to ask you about the picture of the beautiful young maiden whom you have painted on the front of your boat.

VLADIMIR: The beautiful maiden is as brave and kind as she is lovely to look upon, Your Majesty. I know because she is my wife.

KING: And how did you chance to meet her, sir?

VLADIMIR: It was my good fortune. We docked in a port many miles from here and were placed next to a foreign boat. There was such wailing and crying coming from the hold of the ship that I asked to talk to the captain to see what was the matter.

KING: Yes, and what did you learn?

VLADIMIR: That he had a group of persons aboard who were going to be sold as slaves at the market at Istanbul. My future wife and her nurse were among them. I could not let that happen.

QUEEN: Was the name of the nurse Rachel?

VLADIMIR: None other. She is with my wife, Helene, at my parents' home now. They are awaiting our return.

QUEEN: Adolph, I told you it had to be her!

KING: Yes, I know.

VLADIMIR: Her?

KING: Our only daughter, Helene. With her nurse, Rachel, she was kidnapped and taken from us four years ago.

QUEEN: Our little girl! Oh, Adolph, she is safe.

KING: Yes, and we must find a way to make it up to these kind people who have kept her that way.

VLADIMIR: But, Sir, that is not necessary.

KING: It is to me. We must show our gratitude to your family for their kindness to Helene.

QUEEN: And to show my thanks I will send some of my finest jewelry to your mother.

VLADIMIR: That's not necessary.

KING: But we want to do these things. I will send my largest ship loaded with gifts for your parents. Harold, you must prepare to go, too.

HAROLD: Am I to be a gift?

KING: No, you are to give them our personal invitation to come to our country when Helene returns. We want them to stay with us at the palace for as long as they like.

VLADIMIR: We'll be back soon. I know that Helene will want to waste no time in getting here. She's missed you both a great deal and talks about you often.

QUEEN: How wonderful it will be to see our daughter again.

CURTAIN

SCENE VI. The sitting room of Helene's parents.
    There are two chairs, a table, and a sofa. The queen, Vladimir's mother, and Pamela and Deborah are talking.

QUEEN: You don't know how wonderful it is to have our Helene home with us. We were afraid we'd never see her again.

MOTHER: I can imagine. We feel that way about Vladimir, too.

QUEEN: Oh, my dear, I didn't mean to be cruel. In my happiness I forgot about the loss of your son, Vladimir. I'm so sorry.

MOTHER: It's all right. I understand.

PAMELA: He was very special.

DEBORAH: Yes, and so kind to everyone.

MOTHER: And not knowing what could have happened to him makes it worse.

QUEEN: I know.

DEBORAH: He'd spent a lot of time at sea. He knew to stay away from the railing during a storm.

PAMELA: I still can't understand why he was on deck.

MOTHER: But Harold says he saw him there just a little while before they started looking for him.

QUEEN: It is strange.

MOTHER: And so sad. My Vladimir.

QUEEN: Yes. It's terrible for you.

(*Laura enters.*)

LAURA: I've been on a walk around the palace. The grounds are beautiful.

QUEEN: I'm glad you like them. We want you to be happy here. We feel you are part of our family now.

DEBORAH: You make us feel that way.

LAURA: If only we had Vladimir, then everything would be perfect.

MOTHER: We were just talking about him.

LAURA: I guess we all think about him a lot.

(*Helene enters with Harold.*)

HELENE: Mother, where is Father? I've got to find him right away.

QUEEN: In his study, I think, dear. What's so important?

HAROLD: She's all excited over nothing.

HELENE: That's not true.

(*Helene goes to the table, picks up a bell, and rings it. A maid enters.*)

MAID: You rang, Your Majesty?

HELENE: Yes, please go to the study and ask my father to come here immediately.

MAID: Very well. (*She exits.*)

HAROLD: Really, Helene. You shouldn't bother your father on such a silly matter.

HELENE: It's not silly. I know what I saw.

(*Harold puts up his hands as if to say, "How ridiculous!" The king and Vladimir's father enter.*)

KING: Helene, the maid said it was something important. What can I do for you?

HAROLD: Her imagination is playing tricks on her, Your Highness.

KING: I want to hear about it from my daughter. What is it, Helene?

HELENE: Harold and I were just about to come into the gates when a poor beggar came up to the window in the carriage.

KING: Yes?

HELENE: Father, he was wearing Vladimir's ring!

KING: Are you sure?

HELENE: I'd know it anywhere.

FATHER: Was it the one with the rubies that I gave him?

HELEN: Yes, and Father, he may still be out there. Harold made the carriage keep on going.

HAROLD: Of course, I did, Your Majesty. It was for Helene's protection.

HELENE: Please hurry and get the guards. Have them stop everyone out there.

KING: What did he look like?

HELENE: I didn't really see his face. It all happened too fast. But he was wearing ragged white clothes.

HAROLD: That could be anyone.

KING: But only one person would have a ring like that! I'll see what I can do. (*He exits.*)

HELENE: Oh, thank you. I knew you'd help.

(*The others start to talk at once.*)

PAMELA: Do you suppose ...?

DEBORAH: Maybe he'll know something about Vladimir.

MOTHER: Wouldn't it be wonderful if we could find him?

CURTAIN

SCENE VII. A peasant's cottage.
   There are a table and two chairs. Vladimir, dressed in rags, is talking to the old man whom he rescued from the dungeon.

OLD MAN: You really got to see her?

VLADIMIR: Yes, she was riding in a carriage with Harold. Just as I got to the window I saw him sitting by her.

OLD MAN: And . . .

VLADIMIR: They were laughing and talking together.

OLD MAN: It must have been hard for you to see Helene like that with the man who tried to kill you.

VLADIMIR: You should have just left me there on the beach to die.

OLD MAN: You didn't leave me to die in the dungeon.

VLADIMIR: But that was different.

OLD MAN: No, it wasn't.

VLADIMIR: But you had a chance for a new life. I can't even get close to Helene.

OLD MAN: Things will get better. You'll see.

VLADIMIR: I've given up hope. (*There is a loud knocking on the door.*)

OLD MAN: Now who could that be? (*There is another knock.*) Just a minute. I'm coming. Who is it?

1ST GUARD: We're officers from the king. Let us come in.

(*The old man opens the door. Two guards enter.*)

OLD MAN: What do you want?

2ND GUARD: We want to see your hands.

OLD MAN: Our hands?

1ST GUARD: Yes, hold them out. Both of you. (*He looks at the old man's hands. The second guard goes to Vladimir.*)

2ND GUARD: Where did you get this ring?

VLADIMIR: My father gave it to me.

2ND GUARD: Likely story. (*To the 1st guard.*) Come over here. I think we've found what we're looking for.

(*The first guard crosses to Vladimir and looks at his hand.*)

1ST GUARD: I think you're right. I'll go get the others. (*He exits.*)

VLADIMIR: Why are you here?

1ST GUARD: King's orders. We've been looking for everyone who was seen near the palace this afternoon. We were told that a man who lives in this house was there.

(*Helene, Alec, Vladimir's father, and the King enter. Vladimir hangs his head, but Helene rushes over to him. She raises his head and looks at him piercingly.*)

HELENE: Vladimir! It's you. Where have you been? What are you doing in those clothes? (*Alec and Vladimir's father rush to his side and give him a hug.*)

VLADIMIR: I've been here with my friend, Hassan. He found me on the beach almost dead after Harold pushed me overboard in the storm.

ALEC: So that's what happened. I've suspected him all long.

KING: Why would he do that?

VLADIMIR: He said he was supposed to have married Helene and I took her away from him.

FATHER: But it wasn't until after she had been taken as a slave.

HELENE: I wouldn't have married him anyway. Why didn't you come to the palace?

VLADIMIR: I tried to everyday, but nobody would believe my story or let me near the door.

HELENE: Then if you hadn't come to the carriage window and I hadn't seen your ring, I'd never have found you.

VLADIMIR: That's true.

HELENE: Why did you turn your head away?

VLADIMIR: I saw you laughing and talking and I thought that you were happy together.

HELENE: He had just said something funny. I could never be happy with anyone but you.

ALEC: You should have seen her. She cried all the time.

KING: Now it will be Harold's turn. He will pay dearly. I trusted him as a son and he did this vile deed to Helene's husband.

VLADIMIR: And Hassan? May he come? He nursed me back to health and shared what little he had with me.

OLD MAN: Only because you saved my life first when you paid my fine and kept me out of prison.

FATHER: Vladimir did that for you?

OLD MAN: Yes, and others, too.

KING: Then, of course, he must come with us. I will see that he is handsomely rewarded.

VLADIMIR: That's very kind. Thank you.

FATHER: . . . And, Son . . .

VLADIMIR: Yes?

FATHER: I know now that I was wrong.

VLADIMIR: How, Father?

FATHER: Being so angry with you for giving away your cargo instead of making money with it.

HELENE: You understand why he did it?

FATHER: I know that Vladimir is more important to us than all the money in the world.

VLADIMIR: Thank you, Father.

FATHER: Never again will I say it is wrong to do a kind deed.

VLADIMIR: Even when I make bad bargains?

FATHER: Even then. Your two bad bargains are what brought you back to us again.

HELENE: And that's the best thing that could happen to any of us.

FATHER: And we will never forget it.

CURTAIN

GLOSSARY OF THEATER ARTS TERMS

ABOVE—To be further upstage of someone, or away from the audience.

ACT—(*noun*) Division of a play. (*verb*) To portray characters in a scene.

ACT CURTAIN—The curtain that masks the stage from the audience.

ACTION—Movement or business that takes place on stage.

AD LIB—Spur-of-the-moment lines or business improvised by actors.

APRON—The part of the stage that extends out from the proscenium.

AREAS—Divisions of the stage.

ARENA THEATER—Staging where the audience sits on four sides of the actors.

BACKDROP—Upstage curtain painted with a scene.

BATTEN—A pipe from which scenery, lights, or draperies are hung.

BELOW—To be downstage or nearer the audience.

BLOCK—To come between another actor or object and the audience.

BLOCK OUT—Plan the movement and business of a play.

BOX SET—An interior set showing three walls of a room.

BUSINESS—Hand movements.

CAST—The actors in a production.

CASTING—Deciding the roles of the actors.

CENTER STAGE—The area in the middle of the stage.

CHARACTERIZATION—The dramatic representation of a character.

COLOR WHEEL—Located in front of a light. Changes light color when rotated.

COMMUNICATION—The giving and receiving of messages.

COOL-DOWN ACTIVITIES—Relaxing or quieting activities.

COVER—To come between another actor or object and the audience.

CREATIVE DRAMA—Participants are the primary creators. They engage in improvised responses. There is no finished performance before an audience.

CROSS—To move from one place to another on stage.

CUE—The word or business preceding an actor's lines.

CURTAIN CALL—The reappearance of the cast after the final curtain.

CYCLORAMA/CYC—The curtain or curved wall encircling the stage.

DIALOGUE—Interaction between characters to communicate thoughts.

DIMMER—A device for controlling the brightness of lights.

DIRECTOR—One who plans the actions and is in control of rehearsals.

DOWNSTAGE—Section of the stage closest to the audience.

DRESS STAGE—Move unobtrusively to avoid being blocked from view.

EXIT—(*verb*) To leave the stage. (*noun*) An outside door.

FLAT—A wooden frame covered by canvas, masonite, or plywood.

FLOODLIGHTS—Unfocused lights that cover a large area.

FLY—To hang scenery or lighting instruments above the stage.

FOOTLIGHTS—Lights located on the stage floor near the audience.

GELATIN—Colored plastic, glass, or cellophane used in front of a light.

GESTURE—A movement (usually made by the hands) to convey a thought.

HOLD FOR LAUGHS—Wait for laughter to stop before giving a line.

HOUSE—The audience or area in front of the footlights.

HOUSE LIGHTS—Lights for the illumination of the auditorium.

HOUSE MANAGER—Person in charge of activities related to the audience.

IMPROVISATION—The spontaneous actions or speech of an actor.

IN-THE-ROUND—Arena theater. Stage with the audience on all four sides.

INFLECTION—The raising or lowering of the pitch of the voice.

INTERPRETIVE READING—To read in understandable and artistic terms the writings of another person.

LINES—The speeches of actors.

MASK—(*verb*) To go between a person or object and the audience. (*noun*) A face covering.

MOVEMENT—Going from one place to another on stage.

MUGGING—Grimacing, or overdone facial movement.

OFFSTAGE—Areas of the stage not visible to the audience.

OPEN UP—To turn the body toward the audience.

PACE—Rate at which a scene is played.

PANTOMIME—Movement or gestures without words used to convey ideas.

PICK-UP-CUES—Say lines immediately after the cue has been given.

PLACES—The command given to actors to be in position and ready to start a scene.

PLOT—The story of the play.

PROFILE—Side view.

PROJECT—(*verb*) To make the voice heard by the entire audience.

PROMPT—To give an actor a line or word that has been forgotten.

PROMPT BOOK—Book containing play, stage directions, and notes.

PROPS/PROPERTIES—All articles on stage except scenery. Hand props are articles hand-carried by actors, such as glasses, food, etc.

PROSCENIUM—The arch that frames the stage.

PUPPETS—Doll-like figures manipulated by hands or strings.

REHEARSAL—A practice.

RHYTHM—The regular recurrence of beat.

RHYTHMIC MOVEMENT—Activities to a rhythmic pattern.

ROLE—A character in a play.

ROLE-PLAYING—The enacting of a role, or character, other than oneself.

SENSORY AWARENESS—The sharpening of perception and opening of senses to heighten recall.

SENSORY RECALL—To remember sensory experiences in order to recreate them accurately.

SET—The arrangement of flats/scenery to provide a background for the action of the play.

SHADOW PLAY—The use of hands or puppets behind a backlighted sheet.

SIDE-COACHING—Suggestions or comments by a leader to improve the action.

SIGHT LINES—Imaginary lines of sight from the auditorium to the stage that determine what can be seen from the audience.

SPOT/SPOTLIGHT—A focused beam of light covering a relatively small area.

STAGE LEFT—The area of the stage to the actor's left while facing the audience.

STAGE MANAGER—Person responsible for running the performance.

STAGE RIGHT—The area of the stage to the actor's right while facing the audience.

STAY IN CHARACTER—Keep concentration in order to effectively portray a character. Pertains to voice, posture, and movement.

STEAL—To take the audience's attention away from the actor to whom it rightfully belongs.

STRAIGHT PART—A role where an actor portrays a character that is close to his or her own age and type.

STRIKE—To take down and remove a set from the stage.

TEASERS—Curtains hung above the stage behind the act curtain, and used to mask the top of the stage from the audience.

TEMPO—The speed at which a line or scene is played.

THEATER—A building which houses a stage.

THEATER-IN-THE-ROUND—Arena theater. Stage with the audience on all four sides.

THEME—The main idea of a play.

THRUST STAGE—A stage that extends into the auditorium so that the audience sits on three sides of the actors.

TIMING—The delivery of a line or execution of business for maximum dramatic effect.

TORMENTORS—Vertical flats or curtains hung behind the act curtain on either side of the stage to adjust the stage width.

TRYOUTS—An audition. The process which allows actors to read for parts in a play.

UPSTAGE—The area of the stage furthest from the audience. Also, the move upstage of another actor so that the actor must turn away from the audience to establish eye contact with the person being addressed.

WARM-UPS—Activities for limbering up bodies and voices.

WINGS—The areas on either side of the stage.

INDEX

References to illustrations are in boldface.

319

ABOUT THE AUTHOR

Gene Beck received a degree in drama from the University of Texas at Austin and was the only one in her graduating class selected to direct a play for public performance. After graduating, Mrs. Beck became active in community theater and did radio and television work. She has taught in college, elementary, and secondary schools, was selected as an outstanding American Elementary School Teacher, and was elected into membership of Delta Kappa Gamma, an honorary society for educators. Mrs. Beck has served as an educational consultant and conducted workshops in Texas, Oklahoma, Arkansas, Georgia, Ohio, Manitoba, British Columbia, Germany, and Mexico. She was an editor for Economy Publishing Company in Oklahoma City. Gene Beck currently resides and teaches in Chapala, Mexico, where she is a member of the Lake Side Little Theater.